*A Programmer's Guide to*
# FILE PROCESSING

**PWS-KENT SERIES IN COMPUTER SCIENCE**

*FORTRAN 77 and Numerical Methods for Engineers,* Second Edition
   Borse

*Microprocessor Systems Design*
   Clements

*Artificial Intelligence: A Knowledge-Based Approach*
   Firebaugh

*Expert Systems: Principles and Programming*
   Giarratano and Riley

*Using BASIC: An Introduction to Computer Programming,* Third Edition
   Hennefeld

*Using Microsoft and IBM BASIC: An Introduction to Computer
Programming*
   Hennefeld

*Using Turbo Pascal 3.0, 4.0, and 5.0*
   Hennefeld

*Digital Design*
   Johnson and Karim

*Systems Development: Requirements, Evaluation, Design and
Implementation*
   Jordan and Machesky

*Assembly Language for the PDP-11, RT-RSX-UNIX,* Second Edition
   Kapps and Stafford

*VAX Assembly Language*
   Kapps and Stafford

*Data Structures, Algorithms and Program Style*
   Korsh

*Data Structures, Algorithms and Program Style Using C*
   Korsh and Garrett

*A Practical Approach to Operating Systems*
   Lane and Mooney

*Advanced Structured BASIC: File Processing with the IBM-PC*
   Payne

*Structured Programming Using QuickBASIC*
   Payne

*Comprehensive Structured COBOL,* Third Edition
  Popkin

*Advanced Programming and Data Structures Using Pascal*
  Riley

*Data Abstraction and Structure: An Introduction to Computer
Science II*
  Riley

*Programming Using Turbo Pascal*
  Riley

*Using Modula-2*
  Riley

*Using Pascal: An Introduction to Computer Science I*
  Riley

*Programming in BASIC for Engineers*
  Rojiani

*Logic and Structured Design for Computer Programmers*
  Rood

*Structured Programming in Assembly Language for the IBM-PC*
  Runnion

*Problem-Solving Using Pascal: Algorithm Development and
Programming Concepts*
  Skvarcius

*Design and Analysis of Algorithms*
  Smith

*FORTRAN for Scientists and Engineers*
  Weinman

*VAX FORTRAN,* Second Edition
  Weinman

*C Programming*
  Worthington

# A Programmer's Guide to
# FILE PROCESSING

**Douglas L. Cashing**
*St. Bonaventure University*

**PWS-KENT PUBLISHING COMPANY**
*Boston*

**PWS–KENT**
Publishing Company

20 Park Plaza
Boston, Massachusetts 02116

PWS-KENT Publishing Company is a division of Wadsworth, Inc.

*Library of Congress Cataloging-in-Publication Data*

Cashing, Douglas L.
    A programmer's guide to file processing / by Douglas L. Cashing.
      p.    cm.
    Includes bibliographical references and index.
    ISBN 0-534-92567-7
    1. File processing (Computer science)   I. Title.
QA76.9.F53C37   1991
005.74—dc20                            90-23531
                                                 CIP

Printed in the United States of America.
91 92 93 94 95 — 10 9 8 7 6 5 4 3 2 1

Sponsoring Editor   *Jonathan Plant*
Assistant Editor   *Mary Thomas*
Production Editor   *Helen Walden*
Manufacturing Coordinator   *Margaret Sullivan Higgins*
Composition   *Modern Graphics, Inc.*
Interior Design   *Elise Kaiser*
Cover Design   *Helen Walden*
Cover Printer   *Henry N. Sawyer Co., Inc.*
Text Printer/Binder   *The Maple-Vail Book Manufacturing Group*

# CONTENTS

## 3    MAINTAINING SEQUENTIAL FILES    *39*

## 4    MAINTAINING DIRECT ORGANIZATION FILES    *51*

## 5    MAINTAINING INDEX-SEQUENTIAL FILES       79

## 6    SECONDARY KEY ACCESS       *103*

# PREFACE

This textbook is intended for use in a sophomore-level computer science course in data file processing, such as the CS 5 course of the Association for Computing Machinery recommended curriculum published in the March 1979 issue of *Communications of the ACM*. All areas of concern in these recommendations have been addressed in this book, with a depth of presentation that should be reasonable for most colleges and universities. The book assumes that the CS 1 and CS 2 courses (Programming I and II) have been taken as prerequisites to this course, primarily for attaining a reasonable level of programming ability. Key topics from these two prerequisites (such as linked data structures and sorting algorithms) are presented in this text for review purposes, and may be included or omitted from the course as needed.

The book is written in a language-independent manner. The algorithms are presented in pseudocode, and can be programmed in any procedural language (such as Pascal, COBOL, FORTRAN, Modula-2, etc.) with at most minor modifications. This allows greater flexibility in using this book in different circumstances. It also emphasizes the distinction between the underlying concepts of file processing and the implementation of these concepts via computer programs and data structures. By not including actual codes for these algorithms, instructors may assign students the task of coding them as part of the course activity.

In this textbook, we will begin by presenting most of the terminology used in the field of file processing, move to algorithms for maintaining (or updating) the data within these files, and then look at the structures and hardware used to implement these files. We will conclude with an overview of database management systems (seen as a refinement or possible improvement on file processing) and a discussion of sorting. The general progression followed is to move from the point of view of a nontechnical user who needs to know the lingo (Chapter 1), to that of an application programmer doing file maintenance (Chapters 2 through 5), to a software programmer needing to understand the underlying structures (Chapters 5 to 7). Chapters 8 and 9 present material that is somewhat tangential to file processing per se but important for anyone studying this area of computer science.

The order in which the chapters may be covered is flexible. Chapter 1 (terminology) should be presented early. Chapter 2 deals with programming style and reviews material usually covered in the CS 1 and CS 2 courses. It includes sample programs, illustrating good and bad designs, for two of the concepts presented in Chapter 1. If the concept of good program design has been mastered by the students, it may be skimmed or omitted. If students' grasp of good programming style is questionable, this chapter should be covered in detail. Chapters 3 through 5 discuss algorithms for file maintenance and processing from the user's point of view, along with some discussion of underlying data structures. These topics are presented early in the text so that students will have time to complete programming assignments during the semester. Chapters 6 and 7 discuss aspects of file structure implementation of which the user would not normally be aware. These chapters could be presented before Chapter 3 without loss of continuity. Chapter 8 is an overview of database management and discusses trends leading beyond the file processing environment; it could be covered at any point in the semester. Chapter 9 deals with sorting considerations. It was put at the end of the text to allow the thread of file maintenance to remain unbroken through the various types of files. Although it does not really require knowledge of Chapters 3 through 8, the section on pointer sorts might make more sense if presented after Chapters 4 and 5, and the merging and merge-sorting of sequential files will follow more naturally after Chapter 3.

The programming aspects of the text are from the point of view of procedural and functional programming languages. While there are advantages to non-procedural languages, the fact is that procedural programming, in some form, must underlie these languages. Moreover, although it will not be discussed in any real detail here, issues of object-oriented programming are coming to the forefront in computer science and will, in all likelihood, have an impact on how we code for file processing (or for any other computer task) in the not-too-distant future.

It should be mentioned here that the approach taken in this book, particularly in Chapters 3 through 5, is from the point of view of application programmers working in a file processing environment. Although file processing software packages are being developed that will make the programs discussed in these chapters obsolete at the application programming level, the concepts of file maintenance and data retrieval presented here are virtually the same, whether one is writing application programs or software systems. This approach was chosen in the belief that it is easier for students to learn these concepts in the more familiar context of application programming. Once the concepts are learned, they may be applied in any situation in which they are required.

This book, while not as lengthy as some of the other texts on the market, is a comprehensive presentation of all of the important topics for a sophomore-level course in file processing. We hope that this shorter (and hence less expensive) text will be welcomed, and that its use will contribute to a significant experience for the student.

A comprehensive Instructor's Manual is available from PWS-KENT to aid instructors using the book in their classes. In addition to exercise answers, this supplement includes transparency masters of key figures, and a special section containing programming code in Pascal and in COBOL. A bound-in diskette containing these programs is also included. These programs (either the printed code or the diskette) may be copied and distributed to students by instructors who want to bring such material into their teaching of the course.

There are many people to whom I owe a great deal in regard to this project: to my parents for many years of love and support; to my wife Betsy and my son Jason for their continued patience and encouragement; to my students, who have motivated me to revise and rethink the nature of this course over the years; to the staff at PWS-KENT for turning my efforts into this finished product; and to the reviewers for their helpful suggestions. Those who checked this book for correctness and appropriateness are: Ashraful A. Chowdhury, Dekalb College; Diane Delisio, Miami University of Ohio; Linda M. Ott, Michigan Technological University; David C. Rine, George Mason University; and Patricia A. Slaminka, Auburn University. I am also indebted to Loren Stephens, a former student of mine, who did the lion's share of writing the answers to the exercises in the Instructors Manual to accompany this textbook.

Any remaining errors, of course, are entirely the fault of the author. Comments, suggestions, or questions on any of this material are welcomed, and may be addressed to the author at the address below.

*Douglas L. Cashing,* Ph.D.
Department of Mathematics
and Computer Science
St. Bonaventure University
St. Bonaventure, NY 14778

# 1 TERMINOLOGY

**F**ile processing can be defined as the study of the structures and algorithms used to implement, maintain, and access individual data files. In this chapter we will define and explain most of the terms used in file processing. The majority of these terms are simple and straight-forward, and will be discussed in the first section. The concepts of access mode and file organization, with their various options, are com-plicated enough to warrant a section each. We will conclude the chapter with a discussion of data retrieval programs. These terms will cover most of our work for Chapters 3 through 5. The last four chapters of the book will introduce some additional terminology, but the expla-nation of these terms will form the basis of those chapters.

## BASIC TERMS

### Data Groupings

Let us begin by noting that the word "data" is the plural form of the word "datum." Sentences with "data" as the subject should therefore have a plural verb, as in "The data are. . . ." While this may make the language seem somewhat stilted at times, at least in comparison to common usage, we will make an effort to be grammatically correct in our discussions here. We will not be concerned, however, with the distinction between plural and singular where "data" is used as an adjective, as in "data file."

A **data file** is a collection of records, usually all having the same format. This is more restrictive than the definition of a file in general, since files need not have a recognizable record format. For example, this textbook is being written on a microcomputer and each chapter is being stored as a (text) file. Each record of these text files is a line of text, with no standard format or length from one line to another. However, for our study of file processing, we will use the term **file** to mean a data file that has a definite record-by-record organization. In most situations, these records will all have the same format, and hence most likely the same length. There are some situations where variable-length records come into play, but we don't need to worry about those until we look at physical storage considerations in Chapter 7.

A **record** is a collection of data items pertaining to one entity in a file. For example, an inventory file would have one record for each item carried by the company. A payroll file would have one record for each employee.

A **field** is a unit of data that describes one aspect of an entity, such as an employee's name, identification number, or date hired. We will be somewhat careless about the distinction between the characteristic described by a field and the value of that characteristic for a certain entity. For example, "age" could be the property of "how long you have been on this planet" or it could be the value "39" in Sam Smith's personnel record under the age column.

A **key** is a field (or combination of fields) that could be used to identify a certain record of interest. For example, we might need to access employee records by name, so name would be a key field. The **primary key** must be a unique identifier for records in a file, and it should be the first consideration in the ordering of records. Frequently, the common identifiers (such as people's names) are not unique, so we invent identifiers (such as Social Security numbers) that are supposed to be unique to serve as the primary key. Since these invented keys are not always known, we sometimes need to have **secondary keys,** which usually are not unique but are more available. For example, a supervisor might need information on Sam Smith without knowing Sam's Social Security number. "Employee name" would be used as a secondary key to access the record, but further checking might have to be done to be sure we have the right Sam Smith.

## File Types

A **backup file** is a copy of the currently active file. The backup is used as insurance against damage to the working copy of the file. If anything does happen to the operational file (such as accidental deletion), the backup copy can be loaded into the operational version of the file. Of course, the backup file must be recreated periodically to reflect any changes made to the operational version. Anyone who has worked with computers for any length of time has probably experienced both the relief of having a backup and the frustration of not having one when operational files have been lost.

An **archive file** is an older version of the operational file. These files are useful in situations where knowledge of previous data may be needed. For example, if archive files were kept for an employee file, we could check back through them for data on an employee who retired last year.

A **master file** is an operational file containing data of significant value. While modifications may need to be made to the master file periodically, the file itself has a long life expectancy. Examples of typical master files in business situations include personnel files and inventory files.

The other type of file that will be of particular interest in this text is the **transaction file.** This file contains an accumulated list of modification requests to be applied to the master file in the context of **batch processing.** Batch processing, as the name implies, consists of collecting a batch of requests (or tasks) until a designated time and then processing them all, one right after the other. Banks typically process checks and deposits to checking accounts in this manner. The alternative, which is called **interactive processing,** requires the system to process each request as soon as it is given to the system by the user. Handling airline reservations would be an example of interactive processing.

## File Updating

Among the more complicated types of operations in file processing are the **update operations.** These include adding new records to a file, deleting records from a file, and modifying the data in certain fields of records in a file. Update operations for the three major file organizations will be discussed in detail in Chapters 3 through 5.

In applying transactions to a master file, **edit errors** may occur. Edit errors are caused by the presence of invalid data in the transaction and thus can be detected by examining the transaction record by itself. For example, if part numbers in an inventory file are supposed to be between 200 and 700, then a part number of 865 would be invalid and an edit error, as would a part number value of ABC. The important thing to remember is that every edit error can be detected by examining the transaction record in isolation from the master file and other transactions. Edit errors should be printed to an edit error report file as they are detected and before trying to apply them to the master file.

The other type of problem that can occur is called an **update error.** An update error can only be detected when a transaction request is compared to records in the master file. The three main update errors are (1) trying to add a record that has the same primary key value as an existing record, (2) trying to change a nonexisting record, and (3) trying to delete a nonexisting record. Other update errors may result from conditions on the file. For example, in an employee file we may have the restriction that salary cannot be decreased. Under these circumstances, a request to change a salary to a figure lower than what is currently in the master record is an update error. These errors should also be reported as they occur.

One other notion associated with an update operation is an **audit,** which is a report of a successful operation. For example, when a record is deleted from a file, we might wish to report that record to an audit report in case someone might need to check it later on. What is needed in the way of audits depends on the requirements of the user. It should be noted that an audit report is different from an audit trail, or log, that can be kept as a record of which users are trying to access which data. Audit trails are important when dealing with the security of confidential data, but they are not a part of application programming for file maintenance.

## ACCESS MODE

**Access mode** refers to the manner in which a program will locate records within a file, i.e., the mode in which the data from the file will be accessed. The three main access modes are **sequential, random,** and **dynamic,** each of which is explained below. Note that the access mode is a property of the program, not a property of the file, and that different programming languages may use different labels for these access modes.

### Sequential Access Mode

In sequential access, we normally are concerned with input from the file or output to the file, but not both. In the sequential access mode, records are accessed in the order in which they appear, one after the other. For input from the file, the first record is read, then the second, and so on. For output to the file, each record written by the program is placed directly after the last record written.

## Random Access Mode

In the random access mode, a specific primary (or secondary) key value is given and the program attempts to locate and retrieve the corresponding record from the file. Random access allows "immediate" access to the desired data for input or to the proper location for output, avoiding the need to start at the first record and then proceed through the records, one after the other, until the proper spot is found. This access mode is sometimes referred to as "relative access" or "direct access."

## Dynamic Access Mode

The dynamic access mode allows a program to switch back and forth between sequential access and random access as needed by the algorithm. One of the main uses for dynamic access is with progressive overflow, which will be discussed under direct file organization in the next section.

## FILE ORGANIZATION

**File organization** refers to the format in which the computer system stores and maintains records in the file. More precisely, it refers to the type of internal structure(s) created and used by the system when it accesses the records (or record locations) for that file. The three main file organizations are **sequential, index-sequential,** and **direct.** We will explain these organizations in the following paragraphs. They will then be discussed in detail in Chapters 3, 4, and 5, where the update process required by each organization will be considered. Keep in mind that organization is a property of the file, and so the definitions for the possible organizations must be in terms of the file structure, not in terms of how we want to retrieve records from it. Again, each programming language may have its own terms to identify these organizations.

## Sequential File Organization

In a sequential file, records are stored serially, in the order in which they are submitted to the file. Normally we want records to be in order by primary key value, so we need to take steps to add records to the file in this manner. Conceptually, sequential files are the easiest to understand; they are also the easiest for the computer system to manage, although updating data in sequential files is more complex than with other organizations, as we will see in later chapters. The only structure provided by the operating system in most sequential file organizations is the starting position of each record without regard to its contents. Thus, the system can always figure out the location of the next record (as required for sequential access mode), but it cannot determine where to find the record for a given key value (preventing the use of random or dynamic access modes on a sequentially organized file).

## Index-Sequential File Organization

Most operating systems will store the records of an index-sequential file in order by primary key value, so that it resembles a properly set up sequential file. However, the system also maintains a separate index file, much like an index at the end of a textbook, that contains information on the location of data records having certain primary key values. To oversimplify a bit, we can think of this index file as containing records of two fields, one the primary key value, and the other the location of the data record for that primary key value. With this additional file, the system can take a primary key value from the user, search the index file, determine the location of the desired record in the data file, and retrieve that record for the user. In a true index-sequential organization, the index file is "transparent to the user," which is a fancy way of saying that the user does not even need to know of its existence. Since the data records are "in order," we can use sequential access to get records in key order. The index file structure also allows the computer system to apply the random access mode to this file, using a table-lookup type of operation.

## Direct File Organization

In direct organization, there are preestablished locations in the file (which frequently means a predetermined number of locations) where records may be stored. For convenience, we will refer to these locations in the file as "record slots" or just "slots." We need to be careful to distinguish between the record (the contents of the slot) and the slot itself, which is simply a location in the file. The desired location of records in direct organization can be determined in a variety of ways, as discussed in the next few paragraphs.

**Actual Versus Relative Addressing.**   The first choice to be made is based on the nature of the slot identifiers. Slots can be referenced by their location within the machine or physical device (an **actual addressing** scheme) or by their position in the file with respect to the other slots (a **relative addressing** scheme). Expecting programmers and data entry personnel to select the actual machine address for storing a record is rather unreasonable, so virtually all direct organization files will use relative addressing at the application programming level. In view of this, our use of direct organization files will focus on relative addressing. Realize, of course, that the system will have to convert the relative address given by the program into an actual machine address in order to retrieve or store the record.

**Direct Versus Indirect Addressing.**   The second choice has to do with the method by which the location is determined from the primary key. One option is called **direct addressing.** This is an unfortunate choice of words, since "direct" is the name of the organization in general as well as of this option within the organization. However, because it is in common usage, we will stick with convention here. With direct addressing, the desired slot number is the primary key value of the record. **Indirect addressing** allows the user to select a primary key value without regard to desired position; the desired position is then computed from this key value by some specified conversion function. For reasons of economy of space, most direct organization files will use indirect addressing. To illustrate this, suppose that the Internal Revenue Service wants to have a direct organization file of all taxpayers. Since taxpayers are referred to by Social Security number, we can assume that this will be the primary key. Social Security numbers are composed of nine digits, which allows for one billion different values. If the file used direct addressing, it would need space for one billion record slots. Since there are far fewer taxpayers, this file would contain a tremendous amount of unused space, making it terribly inefficient. To avoid this problem, the file would be set up with a more reasonable number of record slots, and the desired slot for any given Social Security number would be computed from the number using a preselected conversion function.

**Hashing.**    Computing the location from the primary key value is called **hashing.** While there is an infinite variety of hashing functions, there are certain standard operations from which most hashing procedures are composed. Of course, nonnumeric keys must first be converted to numeric form, perhaps by using the ASCII code for the characters in the key field. For example, the name SMITH could be changed to numeric form with ASCII codes $S = 123, M = 115, I = 111, T = 124$, and $H = 110$, for a total of 583. Once in numeric form, any combination of the following operations could be used: (1) **digit extraction,** which calls for designated digit positions to be selected from the larger numeric version of the key, not necessarily in the order they originally occurred; (2) **folding,** which involves breaking the numeric key into two or more parts, treating the parts as distinct numbers, and adding them together; and (3) **radix conversion,** which involves interpreting the key value as being in some base other than 10, or converting the base-10 form to an equivalent form in some other base. These procedures can be "mixed and matched" in any variety of ways to produce a hashing function. The location computed by the hashing function is referred to as the **home address** for the record.

  Let's consider some quick examples to illustrate the hashing functions mentioned above. For these examples, we'll take the eight-digit key value 91532467. (1) For digit extraction, suppose the hash function uses the second, seventh, fourth, and fifth digits (from left to right) of the primary key to form the address. Our address would then be 1632. (2) If we use folding and break the primary key into three parts composed of three digits, three digits, and two digits, respectively, we would get $915 + 324 + 67 = 1306$ as our address. (3) If we interpret the number to be base 20 instead of base 10, and just use the final three digits, we would get 7, plus 6 times 20, plus 4 times 20 squared, or $7 + 6(20) + 4(400)$, which is $7 + 120 + 1600 = 1727$.

  The hashing function that seems to be the most frequently used, however, is called **prime division/remainder.** With this hashing function, the primary key value is divided by a predetermined prime number, and the remainder (or the remainder plus 1) is used as the address (or as the input to the next phase of the hashing). A prime number is an integer greater than 1 that is divisible (without a remainder or fractional part) only by itself and by 1. The use of the remainder should bring back memories of elementary school arithmetic, where in division problems we wrote down the largest whole number quotient, and then indicated how much was left over. As an illustration, let's suppose that the prime number we are using is 19, and that our primary key value is 462. Doing the arithmetic, we see that 19 divides into 462 twenty-four times (which is of no concern to us here) with a remainder of 6. Thus the address that we want is either 6 or 7, depending on whether we add 1 to the remainder. The decision whether to add 1 to the remainder depends on the lowest slot number available (either 0 or 1).

Recall that under this integer division, the remainder will be less than the divisor. Thus, in our example above, remainders will be between 0 and 18 inclusive, providing nineteen different addresses. If we assume that we are using relative addressing (you remember that from a few paragraphs back) and that slot numbers begin with 1 (not 0), the example hashing function here will allow us to access slots 1 through 19. From this we see that the prime number to be used should be as large as possible without exceeding the number of home addresses in the file (recalling that direct organization files typically have a predetermined number of slots available). If our divisor is larger than the number of slots, the hash function will produce addresses that are out of range. If our divisor is too small, there will be available slots that we cannot access. Notice that the prime number becomes a property of the file at the time the file is first created, as do the details of any hashing function. This exact hashing function must be incorporated into any program using this file.

In the example above, we saw that 7 was the desired slot number for the record with key value 462 (if slot numbers start at 1). With record 462 safely stored in slot number 7, suppose we need to add a record to the file with primary key value 329. Using the hash function, we again get an address of 7. Two different values that hash to the same slot number are called **synonyms,** and getting two records with synonyms for keys to store in the file is called a **collision.** Any of the hashing functions discussed above will produce synonyms, since they are not one-to-one functions. Thus, before we can conclude our discussion of hashing we must consider ways of dealing with the collisions that will inevitably occur. The two main schemes for this are progressive overflow and chained overflow.

**Progressive Versus Chained Overflow.**   In progressive overflow, a new record whose home address is already occupied will be placed in the next available slot in the file. To search for a record, we start with the home address, as computed from the desired key value. If the record is not in that slot, we check slots sequentially until we find the record or until all slots have been checked. We must remember that in checking slots, either for open space for a new record or to retrieve an existing record, the slot number must be reset to 1 (or 0) when we get to the highest slot number. We must also remember to stop when we get back to the home address, because this means that there is no open space to add (an update error specific to direct organization files) or that the record we wanted to retrieve is not in the file. Notice the use of the dynamic access mode (random access of the home slot, followed by sequential access of the other slots to be checked).

Chained overflow employs a separate overflow area to handle collisions. In other words, the file is divided logically into two sections, one exclusively for home addresses and the other exclusively for synonyms of existing records. The hashing function should produce addresses in the home address section only. If the home address for a new record is already in use, the new record is put into a slot in the overflow area. This slot is then connected to the chain of all records having that home address. The usual data structure for this is the **linked list,** which will be reviewed in Chapter 4. Notice that while the logical design of chained overflow seems more complex than that of progressive overflow (at least for those who are not well versed in linked data structures), the operation will be more efficient. With chained overflow, home addresses always hold a record that hashed to that address (unless the slot is empty, of course). In progressive overflow, a home address might well have an overflow record that hashed to an entirely different home address. When trying to retrieve a record under chained overflow, we need only check slots of records that are synonyms of the desired record. In progressive overflow, we might end up checking every slot in the file, particularly if the requested record is not actually there. For this reason, we will focus on chained overflow to handle collisions.

Notice that direct organization files can accommodate either sequential access or random access. Since record slots are in order by slot number, a program can start at the beginning and move slot by slot through the file. Realize that this sequence does not necessarily correspond to the primary key order of the records, however. On the other hand, once a slot number is determined (by using the primary key value directly or indirectly), the program can retrieve the contents of that slot without having to access any other slots in the file. Thus the random access is provided by a computation on (or examination of) the key to determine the location to access.

# RETRIEVAL PROGRAMS

## Report Generation

**Report generation** is the term commonly used for the batch type of retrieval operation. In such a situation, the program will normally check each record of the file in a sequential access mode. As each record is read into the program, it will be handled according to the specifications of the task. If the report is to include all records of the file, the record will be formatted and sent to the output file. If only certain records are to be reported, the record will be tested against specified criteria before being sent to output. If the report is merely a summary, the necessary information will be combined with the information gathered from the other records that have been read and processed. The main point is that a report generation program works without user intervention, checking all records of the file in sequential order. An example of a report generation program will be given at the end of Chapter 2, where we will illustrate good and bad programming styles.

## Query Programs

A **query program,** on the other hand, is interactive. The user responds to a program prompt by entering the data needed to specify the record or records desired. The program will retrieve that record (or records) and display them to the user. Normally this cycle of prompt, user input, retrieval, and display will be repeated until the user enters a special code to terminate the execution of the program. The label "query program" is somewhat misleading, since it can also denote interactive programs that modify the data in the file, rather than simply answer questions about the data in the file. A sample query program will be included at the end of Chapter 2 in our illustration of programming style issues.

# CONCLUDING REMARKS

This chapter has presented most of the terminology needed in the study of file processing. The student is urged to review these terms carefully, since they will be used throughout the rest of this text. Understanding the definitions at this time will save a good deal of time and effort later on. Particular attention should be paid to the distinction between access mode and file organization, as this is a very common source of confusion.

Please note also that common usage of this terminology is not always consistent. Other authors and practitioners may use these terms in slightly different ways than we have presented them, and not always in agreement with each other. But with a good understanding of the way the terms are used here and close attention to context in the future, it should be easy to figure out the true intent of another's language and terminology.

## EXERCISES

1. Review all of the terms presented in this chapter. Be able to explain them in your own words.

2. Formulate some ideas and examples as to when each of the three file organizations would be the most desirable.

3. Formulate some examples of situations in which each of the three access modes would be the most desirable.

4. Consult your dictionary to determine the difference between validity and correctness. Is it possible for a data value to be valid but not correct? Can a data value be correct but not valid?

5. If all the retrieval from a file was to be report generation, which organization would be most appropriate?

6. If all the retrieval from a file was to be query processing, which organization would be most appropriate?

7. If some of the retrieval was query processing and some was report generation, and the report was to be in order by primary key, which organization would be most appropriate?

8. Give some examples (other than those given in the chapter) of situations where access by secondary key value would be needed.

# 2 PROGRAMMING STYLE

Although this text is not intended to be a book on programming, it is a book for programmers. And although the emphasis is on understanding file structure and usage, anyone using this book will need to write programs to develop a full understanding of these concepts. The objective of this chapter is to ensure that good programming style is used in designing and implementing these file processing programs.

The ideas presented here should have been developed in the first and second programming courses that are assumed as prerequisites for a course in file processing. If this actually happened, then this chapter may be skimmed or omitted altogether. On the other hand, if these topics were not properly understood, then this chapter should be studied carefully.

## CHARACTERISTICS OF A "GOOD" PROGRAM

While there is room for debate as to what really makes a program "good," there are five main traits that we should consider here. While there may be discussion as to the order of importance of these traits, the arrangement given here is at least reasonable. Let's then consider each trait in turn, beginning with the most important.

1. *The program should work correctly.* The source code typed in to the computer should compile without error, the object code produced should run without crashing, and the output of the program should be correct for any reasonable set of input values. If the program does not have these characteristics, it is not finished. Giving the program over to the user in an unfinished form will cause the user to experience frustration, resentment, and loss of confidence in your abilities. Whether the user is your employer, your client, or your instructor, this is not a good situation.

**2.** *The program should be easy to maintain.* More and more, those involved in computer processing are realizing the need for maintainable program code. No matter how carefully a program is designed, the specifications for the program will eventually change. Even if the original programmer is still available, the understanding of the code will most likely have been forgotten. In order to modify program code to accommodate new specifications, a programmer will need to be able to read the code without a prior knowledge of its content, decipher variable names, come to an understanding of its logic, and then make the necessary adjustments. As more and more programs are written, there is less of a need to develop new programs and more of a need to maintain existing programs. An increasingly higher percentage of programmer time each year is spent on maintenance. (An estimate made in the mid-1980s indicated that 45 percent of all programmer time was spent on modifying existing code, rather than creating new programs. It is likely that percentage has grown significantly since then.) Even if the program you are writing is not one that you plan to keep for any length of time, realize that the maintenance process is very similar to the debugging process, and that program features that facilitate adaptive maintenance and reusability will help with corrective maintenance. Writing maintainable code will make your debugging easier.

**3.** *The program should be user-friendly.* Basically, the user should be pleased with the way the program "interacts" with the outside world. Any information needed by the program should be requested with prompts that are clear, complete, concise, and easy to read. The information produced by the program should be formatted in an orderly and meaningful manner.

**4.** *The program should be robust.* The program should be able to recover from errors resulting from improper usage. Some examples of improper usage include getting nonnumeric input for a numeric variable, trying to open a nonexistent input file, dividing by zero, or using an array index that is out of bounds. Circumstances such as these will normally cause a program to crash during execution unless code is specifically designed to detect and handle them. One must remember that no matter how user-friendly the program, sooner or later some user is going to make a mistake. The program needs reasonable protection against these user errors.

**5.** *The program should be efficient.* Computer resources are expensive, so programs should make the best possible use of them. The two main concerns are storage space and run time. Extra code, including superfluous documentation, requires more space to hold the program. Extra variables also use more space in main memory during execution. Extraneous operations will slow down the execution of the program, increasing the response time and delaying other jobs on the system.

## ATTAINING THESE CHARACTERISTICS

Several of the characteristics mentioned above can be attained in a fairly straightforward manner, once the characteristics are understood. One makes a program user-friendly by providing good prompts and well-organized output. One provides robustness by anticipating improper use and writing error-handling code to detect these situations and to recover from them. One makes the program efficient by minimizing the number of variables and the amount of code. Correctness and maintainability are more complex, and will be discussed in detail later in this chapter.

We need to realize that these objectives are somewhat incompatible. Efforts made to attain one of them may detract from another. For example, including error-handling routines will make the program more robust but less efficient. We can make the program more efficient by reusing variable names from an earlier part of the program for new data items, but this makes the program harder to maintain. Thus we need to set our priorities and write our code with these objectives in mind.

### Correctness

Proving beyond a shadow of a doubt that a program is correct is virtually impossible. However, there are several steps that can be taken to increase the likelihood of correctness, and to provide a reasonable amount of evidence that this is the case. We should note that, while program testing is an important activity, such testing can only prove the existence of bugs; it cannot prove that no bugs exist. Proper testing should use data that will test every line of code in the program under all reasonable combinations of circumstances that the program will have to face when put into operation. This may, of course, mean that several sets of test data will have to be chosen, and that the program will have to be run several times, once on each data set. (For purposes of maintainability, these sets of test data should become part of the program's external documentation, to be used in testing any modifications to the code at a later date.) If the program malfunctions under any of these tests, we have proof that a bug exists in the code. But if no error is detected, it might mean only that our testing is incomplete; the circumstance that will lead to a program failure may not occur until after the code is put into operation. Only when testing is sufficiently thorough can we interpret "no errors" as proof of a bug-free program, but this requires "proof" that the test data was exhaustive enough.

Even before we reach the testing phase, there are several important factors to consider. First, we need a correct algorithm for our code. In large part, this is a design issue that can be handled quite nicely in the top-down design to be discussed later. Second, an attitude of intentional error-free coding can go a long way toward eliminating program bugs. It used to be a common attitude among programmers that we should get something into code and then worry about correcting it. This attitude led to quick first versions of programs that then had to undergo agonizing processes of debugging. If we strive for correctness right from the beginning, the overall process can be shortened considerably. Third, in more complex systems creation, we can appeal to correctness proofs. These mathematical techniques of program verification are valuable tools that can be used to build correctness into our programs, but because they are quite technical, they are beyond the scope of this text.

When generating code, we can anticipate the testing and debugging process by including tracing code. Such code displays messages and data values to the programmer as the code executes, including information as to which block of code is being executed at any given time, which facilitates locating the source of any error that does occur. Of course, such tracing commands should not affect the program's data values or its flow of control. The tracing statements should also stand out from the regular code so that they can be easily identified and removed after the code is debugged and before it is put into operation. Many of the more sophisticated programming environments now have a symbolic debugging feature, which reduces or eliminates the need for these tracing commands in the source code.

## Maintainability

Let us now consider the issue of maintainability. Several factors are involved in developing programs that can be easily modified. We basically need code that is easy to read and understand. This can be done by: (1) choosing meaningful, user-defined names for variables and modules; (2) using preset variables (or constants, if the language supports them) for values that do not change during execution of the program (i.e., defining a variable SALES-TAX and assigning it the value 0.06, then using SALES-TAX in computations instead of 0.06); (3) including comments in the code to identify and explain any variable or module names that are not self-explanatory; (4) writing internal (and external) documentation for any code whose function and operation are not obvious; (5) indenting statement lines to emphasize the control structures and the blocks of code under their direction; (6) using blank lines (or white space) to separate blocks of code from each other; (7) limiting the number of lines in each block so that the entire block of code fits on one screen; and (8) structuring the code in a meaningful way. This last point is complex enough to warrant the next two sections for clarification. Realize that when we produce a program that is easy to maintain, we also produce a program that is more likely to be correct and that will be much easier to debug if it is not correct.

## THE STRUCTURE THEOREM

In 1966, Corrado Bohm and Guiseppe Jacopini published a mathematical result in *Communications of the ACM* that we will refer to as the structure theorem. The actual publication is extremely technical, but the theorem can be paraphrased as follows:

> Any program can be written using only the control structures of sequence, selection, and either form of indefinite iteration.

We will consider the details of these control structures in a later paragraph, but first let us consider the implications of the theorem. At first glance, it says that if we have these three control structures available, we don't need any others. The most obvious omission from this list is the branching structure, which is usually implemented in programming languages as the GOTO statement. This is why structured programming is sometimes referred to as GOTO-less programming, which, as we will see, is a gross oversimplification, but still an important characteristic, of structured programming. Realize that branching can occur with other forms of syntax, such as the conditional branch in BASIC (IF N > 0 THEN 590), or the mid-loop exit of the newer languages (such as C's BREAK command).

It follows, then, that if a programming language does not have all three of these control structures, others (such as branching) will need to be included in order to accomplish certain tasks. Pascal, COBOL, and PL/I include all three control structures, and so do not require branching. (COBOL does not have any way of terminating a SECTION except to drop out of the last statement, so branching could be used, but only from the end of a main-level control module—a term that will be explained in the section on top-down design—to the bottom of the code listing.) FORTRAN does not have an indefinite iteration structure, and while FORTRAN 77 has implemented the selection with the BLOCK-IF statement, FORTRAN IV has to use conditional branching to implement selection. In any event, at the design level we are free to write selection and iteration structures, so we can avoid branching at the design stage. If the language in which the design is to be coded does not support selection or iteration, we can use conditional and unconditional branching to simulate these structures, realizing that the branching is inherently there in the structure. This simulation will be more obvious after we explain the control structures.

We must also recognize that just because a structure is not mentioned in the theorem does not mean that it *must* be avoided. The case for avoiding branching has been argued for some time now, starting with E. Dijkstra's letter in *Communications of the ACM* entitled "GOTO Statement Considered Harmful." The theorem itself says simply that we do not need branching; other arguments (such as Dijkstra's letter) are required to claim that we should not use it. Another control structure that is not mentioned in the theorem (and hence is not needed to accomplish programming tasks) but that should be used in coding is the invoking of submodules, such as Pascal's procedures, the subroutine calls of FORTRAN, BASIC, or PL/I, and the modules of Modula-2 and Ada. The use of submodules will be discussed in the next section. The control structures mentioned in the structure theorem are used within each module to control the execution of that block of code. (Note that we are using the word "module" in a generic sense here, and that certain languages use other terms, such as "subroutine" or "procedure," for this concept. Also, some languages, such as Ada and Modula-2, have a more restrictive definition of "module" than what we are using here.)

Let us now consider the control structures mentioned in the theorem. First, we need to know that a control structure is a statement that determines what to do next during execution. The sequence control structure (which is the default condition, and hence is not actually a separate statement in the code) passes control onto the next statement in sequence, reading down the page in the program listing. This is diagrammed in the flowchart shown in Figure 2.1(a).

**FIGURE 2.1(a)** *Sequence Control Structure*

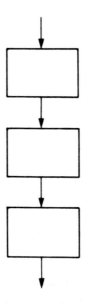

The selection control structure tests a specified condition to choose which option to execute. If the condition is true, one block of code is executed. If the condition is false, then either another block is executed or nothing is done. The standard example of this structure is the IF . . . THEN . . . (ELSE . . . ) statement, in which the ELSE clause is optional. The basic form of the selection is shown in Figure 2.1(b). Some programming languages have extended the selection structure to allow for more than two options, usually as a CASE statement.

Indefinite iteration involves a block of code that may have to be executed several times. The decision whether to execute is based on the testing of a logical condition. There are two variations of indefinite iteration: test-first iteration checks the condition before each pass through the body of the loop, while test-last iteration checks the condition after each pass. The performance of these two variations is the same once the block of code inside the loop is actually entered. The difference is that the test-first iteration might not enter the body at all, since it checks the condition before the first pass. However, the test-last iteration will execute the body at least once, since it does not look at the

**FIGURE 2.1(b)**  *Selection Control Structure*

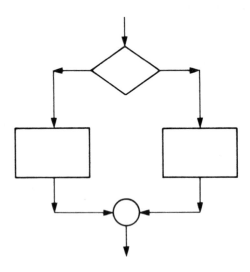

condition until it has completed a pass. Figures 2.1(c) and 2.1(d) illustrate these control structures.

Three points of clarification are probably in order here. First,
indefinite iteration is more flexible than definite iteration, which sets
the exact number of passes that are to be made just before the first
pass is actually done. The FOR-loops of Pascal and BASIC and the

**FIGURE 2.1(c)**  *Test-First Iteration Control Structure*

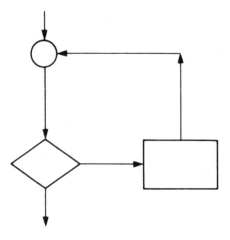

**FIGURE 2.1(d)**   *Test-Last Iteration Control Structure*

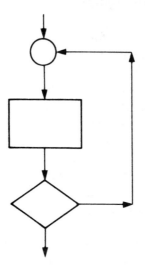

(counted) DO-loops of FORTRAN and PL/I are examples of definite iteration. Indefinite iteration allows for an unpredictable number of repetitions, permitting the body of the loop to trigger its exit condition at the proper time in the execution cycle. This increased flexibility is a two-edged sword, however, because there is also the possibility of an infinite loop.

Second, some authors identify these loops as WHILE and UNTIL loops, rather than as test-first and test-last. This is somewhat misleading, since WHILE and UNTIL refer to whether the condition should be true or false (respectively) in order to execute the body of the loop again, and do not indicate the location of the test relative to the body. If we wish to incorporate this distinction also, we get four types of loops: Do-While and Do-Until are test-last, and While-Do and Until-Do are test-first.

Third, the syntax of a language may not indicate whether the looping is test-first or test-last. This often occurs with the definite iteration structure. FORTRAN 77's DO-loop is test-first, while FORTRAN IV's Do-loop is test-last, even though the syntax is identical. In some cases, the syntax is actually misleading. COBOL implements iteration with a statement of the form PERFORM paragraph-name UNTIL condition, which reads as though it is a test-last statement. However, the run-time module checks the condition before performing the paragraph, making it a test-first structure.

## TOP-DOWN DESIGN/STEPWISE REFINEMENT

The structure theorem discussed above formed the original idea of structured programming. Since that time, however, structured programming has been expanded to also encompass the notions of top-down design and stepwise refinement. Technically, stepwise refinement is a process and top-down design is the resulting product. However, we will follow the fairly common practice of referring to both the process and the result as top-down design, with the context determining the meaning.

In 1956, George Miller stated that an individual can keep approximately seven main ideas in mind at one time. Since many tasks involve significantly more than seven ideas, we need a way of organizing details into manageable units. This is the basis of top-down design, in which we focus on one unit of the task at a time and keep the number of ideas in that unit to seven (more or less). Details not associated with the unit currently being considered are ignored. Such details are included in some other unit of the task and will be brought to mind only when that unit is considered. Units that contain more than seven ideas must have these ideas grouped into blocks and labeled, so that when we consider the unit we bring to mind only these labels rather than all the details the labels represent. Of course, the number of such blocks should be (more or less) equal to seven.

Simply put, the idea of top-down design is to take the overall programming task (which is probably quite complex) and identify its main logical components. Each of these components is then considered in turn. If a component is still complicated, it is broken up into its logical components. This process continues until each component is either decomposed into more components (at a finer level of detail) or is simple enough to understand without further decomposition. This will result in an organization of the programming task into modules, similar to the organization of a company into departments. The organization can be illustrated very nicely by means of a structure chart. In short, for top-down design, we consider the overall logic of our task, ignoring the petty little details as long as possible. Let us assume that one of the subtasks is the storage of data in some particular data structure. By setting up a separate module to oversee these data and to provide all necessary access functions to them, we can properly modularize the program.

Before we consider the benefits of this process, let us look at an example. Suppose we have the task of designing a program to handle the payroll of a company. Since this is an overwhelming task if viewed in its entirety, we break it up into components as follows. For each employee, we will need to get the payroll record, then compute the gross pay, compute the federal withholding, compute the state withholding, compute the other deductions, update the payroll record, and finally print the paycheck. There will be some preliminary initialization to do before processing begins, and some wrap-up after all employees are processed. While this might not be a complete decomposition, it is adequate to demonstrate the process.

Some of these components are apt to be simple enough to understand without further decomposition, such as initialization, wrap-up, and get payroll record. Others probably require further decomposition in order to be manageable. For example, computing gross pay involves either computing for hourly or computing for salaried. When we compute for hourly, we need to compute regular time and compute overtime. To compute federal withholding, we might need to get the number of exemptions and do a federal tax-table lookup. And so it goes, with each operation being examined in turn and decomposed into its logical components if it is too complicated to grasp in its original form. The resulting partial structure chart for this task is shown in Figure 2.2. Once these modules have been identified, we can use pseudocode to specify the mechanics of the operations that are to take place within each of them. After that step has been made, generating program code (in any language) should be reasonably straightforward.

Let us now resume our discussion of top-down design in general. Once the decomposition is complete, we have the program task modularized into manageable units. If we have done a good job with the decomposition, there are a number of features that we should be able to observe. First and foremost, each module should have a single, well-defined role to play in carrying out the task of the program. Perhaps the most useful test for a good decomposition is the ability to select a short but descriptive name for each module. If a name does not spring to mind for a certain module in your structure chart, you probably should back up a step or two and rework the decomposition.

If we have obtained this primary goal in the top-down design, our modules should have several secondary characteristics. First, modules toward the top of the chart should have very little executable code, since their function is to control and direct. These upper-level modules should consist mainly of selection and iteration structures, along with invocation calls to lower-level modules. The actual execution of the programming task will be done in the modules toward the bottom of

**FIGURE 2.2** *Partial Structure Chart for the Payroll Operation*

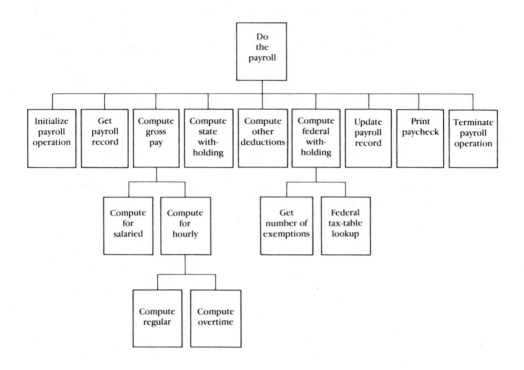

the chart. This corresponds to a company's organization chart, with the chief executive office (CEO) at the top, a row of vice presidents just underneath, and so on down to the blue-collar workers. The CEO and the vice presidents do not do any of the actual work of producing goods, but they make decisions as to what needs to be done and pass these decisions down the chain of command to those responsible for carrying them out.

Second, since each module has a single, specific task, it should have just one entry point (and probably just one exit point). There should be no reason to jump into the middle of a module, since this represents an external decision to skip over part of the module's operation. Exiting from the middle of a module by means of some mid-loop exit command might be reasonable, but this can be handled just as easily by putting the final part of the module inside a selection statement.

Third, we should have modules that possess high levels of cohesion, meaning that each module should have a single, well-defined purpose and all the code inside the module should contribute to that purpose, and to that purpose only.

Finally, the modules should be loosely coupled. This is a fancy term for having each pair of modules as independent of each other as possible. The operations of one module should affect the operations of another module only through some data element that they share explicitly by passing it back and forth. We want to avoid the "side effects" of one module changing a data value that is used somewhere else, unbeknown to a programmer reading the code.

Care should be taken not to view top-down design as a one-pass operation. In practice, as the decomposition progresses, it may become apparent that improper choices were made previously, requiring a return to a higher level in order to make some adjustments before working back down. Thus, while the general flow of development is from the top down, there will be times where some bottom-up work will occur.

Before leaving this topic, it should be mentioned that there tends to be some reluctance to do top-down design. The process certainly takes time and delays us from typing code into the computer. Why should we dilly-dally around with this when there are deadlines to meet? The answer is that the time invested in a good top-down design will more than pay for itself when we get to the testing and debugging stage. Identifying errors, locating the incorrect code, and making the corrections are much easier if the program has been well modularized. The project will actually be completed sooner if we invest the time and effort up front to design the program well.

―――――

## TOP-DOWN VERSUS BOTTOM-UP CODING

Once the design has been completed, we are ready to implement that design in program code. There are two approaches to this coding: top-down and bottom-up. From our discussion of top-down design, it should be fairly obvious that for top-down coding, we start at the top (most general) level of our design and write modules of program code for each module in the structure chart. It should also be clear that bottom-up coding will start with the modules at the bottom of the structure chart, code the most specific details first, then work up to the upper-level control modules.

If we take the top-down approach to coding, it is helpful to use what are called "stubs" for the lower-level modules. The approach is to write the code for the selection, iteration, and module calls in the top-level modules. We then create the blocks for the lower-level modules, but with only enough code to let us know when the module has been invoked (and perhaps what data it received). Our program at this time will not actually perform the task assigned, but it will show us whether our control logic is correct (and deal with compile errors at the main level). By compiling and executing this partial program, we can deal with testing and debugging in smaller units than if we wait until the full program is coded. The report messages in the stubs will play the role of trace commands as the code is expanded. Once we are satisfied with the modules that have been coded, we select more modules, code them, then re-compile and test them. Thus, we may go through several successful but incomplete trial runs before we arrive at the full-scale program. However, the time and effort of multiple (though partial) testing usually pays off in reduced total time for debugging.

With the bottom-up approach, we also go through several stages of compiling and testing partial code. Here, however, the early stages test the logic of the highly specific but limited-scope modules at the lowest levels of the design. When we are convinced that these modules are working correctly, we can add the modules above them to invoke these tasks at the proper time. This approach is a bit more difficult in practice than top-down coding because of the issues of control and invocation. One way to handle the control problem is to write these low-level modules as separate programs, compile and test them in this form, and then copy them into the main program (with enough editing to convert them from stand-alone programs into procedures or subroutines). The other approach is to write the higher-level modules as stubs. These stubs would include enough code to invoke the lower-level modules, but without concern as to when, how often, or under what circumstances to invoke them. In practice, it might even be reasonable to use some combination of top-down and bottom-up coding. The main idea is to compile and test the program in portions, as you generate code, rather than wait until all code is generated before trying any of it.

## EXAMPLES: BOTH GOOD AND BAD

### A Report Generation Programming Task

Let us consider the task of reading through an inventory file to see which items need to be reordered. The file will contain the name of each item in the first ten columns, then the quantity in stock, and then the level at which the item should be reordered. (In practice, such a file would have several other fields as well, but those fields are of no interest for this example.) The vice president for inventory control has decided that the names of items that are at or below the reorder point should be printed to another file, which can be sent to the line printer for a hard copy. This file should have no more than forty items per page, with a brief heading and a page number at the top of each page. The program should display the number of items to be reordered at the terminal from which it was executed.

Below are two Pascal programs written to accomplish this task. The purpose of including these examples here is not to teach you the syntax and grammar of Pascal, but to emphasize the techniques of good programming style. Both programs have been tested and work correctly. The compiling and execution took place on a Prime-750 computer using Sheffield Pascal, but except for opening the files and the input-output commands on the files, the code is all ANSI standard Pascal and should run on any system (once the file I/O syntax is properly modified). As you read these programs, see if you can identify the good and bad stylistic features of each.

First, the "good" example:

```
Program Reorder(inv_file, reorder_file, output);

const lines_per_page = 40;
      page_feed_code = 12;

var   inv_file, reorder_file : text;
      name : string [10];
      quant : integer;
      reorder_point : integer;
      lines_printed : integer;
      page_num : integer;
      reorder_count : integer;
      item_out : boolean;

Procedure Initialize (var lines_printed,
            page_num, reorder_count : integer);

begin
   reset (inv_file);
   rewrite (reorder_file);
   lines_printed := lines_per_page; {to trigger
                              1st page heading}
   page_num := 0;
   reorder_count := 0;
   writeln (output, 'working...');
end; {Initialize}
```

```
Procedure Check_Inv (quant, reorder_point :
                                        integer;
                    var needed : boolean;
                    var reorder_count:integer);

begin
   if quant > reorder_point
      then   needed := false
      else   begin
                needed := true;
                reorder_count :=
                                reorder_count + 1;
             end;   {else clause}
end;   {Check_Inv}




Procedure Check_Inv (quant, reorder_point :
                                        integer;
                    var needed : boolean;
                    var reorder_count:integer);

begin
   page_num := page_num + 1;
   writeln (reorder_file, chr(page_feed_code));
   write (reorder_file, 'Items to be
                              reordered        ');
   writeln (reorder_file, 'Page # ',
                                    page_num:3);
   writeln (reorder_file);
   lines_printed := 0;
end;   {New_Page}




Procedure Write_Reorder (var page_num,
      lines_printed : integer; name : string);

begin
   if lines_printed = lines_per_page
      then New_Page (page_num, lines_printed);
   writeln (reorder_file, name);
   lines_printed := lines_printed + 1;
end;   {Write_Reorder}
```

```
Procedure Wrap_Up (reorder_count : integer);

begin
   close (inv_file);
   close (reorder_file);
   writeln (output, reorder_count:4, ' items to
                                be reordered');
end;  {Wrap_Up}



begin   {main program}
   Initialize (lines_printed, page_num,
                              reorder_count);
   while not (eof (inv_file)) do begin
       readln (inv_file, name, quant,
                              reorder_point);
          Check_Inv (quant, reorder_point,
                         item_out, reorder_count);
          if   item_out
              then Write_Reorder (page_num,
                              lines_printed, name);
   end;  {while loop}
   Wrap_Up (reorder_count);
end.
```

And now, the "bad" example:

```
Program Reorder (infile, outfile, output);
    var infile, outfile : text; n : string [10];
        q : integer; rp : integer; lp : integer;
                  pn : integer; rc : integer;
begin
   reset (infile);
   rewrite (outfile);
   lp := 40;
   pn := 0;
   rc := 0;
   while not (eof (infile)) do begin
   readln (infile, n, q, rp);
   if   q <= rp
   then  begin
   if   lp = 40
   then  begin
   pn := pn + 1;
   writeln (outfile, chr(12));
   write (outfile, 'Items to be reordered  ');
   writeln (outfile, 'Page # ', pn:3);
```

```
            writeln (outfile);
            lp := 0;
            end;
            writeln (outfile, n);
            rc := rc + 1;
            lp := lp + 1;
            end;
            end;
            close (infile);
            close (outfile);
            writeln (output, rc:4, ' items to be
                                        reordered');
    end.
```

A few comments are probably in order here. First, the modularization in the first example might appear to be overdone. However, the idea was to demonstrate the identification of individual component tasks and the separation of these tasks into distinct modules in the code. In fact, the modularization is underdone, since the Initialization procedure and the Wrap-Up procedure each contain two distinct functions. To truly complete the separation of functions, we would need modules to open files, set initial values, close files, and report summary information.

Second, the "bad" example might also seem to be extreme. Again, the purpose was to emphasize problems with poorly structured code. There are no "problems" with that listing that have not appeared in students' assignments at one time or another.

Keeping in mind that both programs work correctly, we should note that the second program is more efficient. The code occupies less space in memory, uses fewer variables, and runs faster than the first program. However, which program would you rather have to work on if you were responsible for program maintenance?

## A Query Processing Task

Let us now suppose the programming task is to write a program that will prompt the user for the name of an inventory item. If that name identifies a record in the file, then the information on that item is displayed to the user. Otherwise, the message shown to the user indicates that a nonexisting name has been requested. If the item is in the file and needs to be reordered, that information will be appended to the data displayed. This process will repeat until the user enters a blank name, at which time the program will terminate.

Again, realize that the purpose of these examples is not to force you to become familiar with COBOL programming, but to illustrate and reinforce the ideas of good programming style. In a well-written program, you should be able to follow the operation of the code, even if you are not familiar with the programming language being used.

Both programs were compiled and executed on a Prime-750 computer, using Prime's COBOL compiler. However, with some slight modifications to the ENVIRONMENT DIVISION, these programs should execute correctly on any system using COBOL.

Let's start with the "bad" example this time:

```
IDENTIFICATION DIVISION.
PROGRAM-ID.     QUERY-INV.
ENVIRONMENT DIVISION.
CONFIGURATION SECTION.
SOURCE-COMPUTER.  PRIME-750.
OBJECT-COMPUTER.  PRIME-750.
INPUT-OUTPUT SECTION.
FILE-CONTROL.
    SELECT INF  ASSIGN TO PFMS  ORGANIZATION IS
    INDEXED ACCESS MODE RANDOM RECORD KEY NAME.
DATA DIVISION.
FILE SECTION.
FD  INF RECORD CONTAINS 16 CHARACTERS.
1   INR.
    5   NAME  PIC X(10).
    5   QUANT  PIC 999.
    5   RP PIC 999.
WORKING-STORAGE SECTION.
1   DR.
    5   N-OUT  PIC X(10).
    5   FILLER  PIC X(3)  VALUE SPACES.
    5   Q-OUT  PIC 999.
    5   FILLER  PIC X(5)  VALUE SPACES.
    5   R-OUT  PIC 999.
    5   FILLER  PIC X(5)  VALUE SPACES.
    5   MES PIC X(20).
1   FLAGS.
    5   FF  PIC XXX.
PROCEDURE DIVISION.
CNTL.
    OPEN INPUT INF.
    DISPLAY 'ENTER NAME OR PRESS <RETURN>'.
    ACCEPT N-OUT.
    PERFORM PROC UNTIL N-OUT = '            '.
    CLOSE INF.
    STOP RUN.
```

```
PROC.
    MOVE 'YES' TO FF.
    MOVE N-OUT TO NAME.
    READ INF INVALID KEY MOVE 'NO' TO FF.
    IF FF = 'YES' THEN PERFORM S-REC ELSE
    DISPLAY N-OUT, ' IS NOT AN ITEM NAME ON
                                     FILE.'.
    DISPLAY 'ENTER NAME OR PRESS <RETURN>'.
    ACCEPT N-OUT.
S-REC.
    MOVE NAME TO N-OUT.
    MOVE QUANT TO Q-OUT.
    MOVE RP TO R-OUT.
    IF QUANT > RP THEN MOVE SPACES
    TO MES ELSE MOVE 'NEEDS REORDERING' TO MES.
    DISPLAY DR.
```

And now, the "good" example:

```
IDENTIFICATION DIVISION.
PROGRAM-ID.    QUERY-INV.
*
*
ENVIRONMENT DIVISION.
*
CONFIGURATION SECTION.
*
SOURCE-COMPUTER.   PRIME-750.
OBJECT-COMPUTER.   PRIME-750.
*
INPUT-OUTPUT SECTION.
*
FILE-CONTROL.
    SELECT INV-FILE
        ASSIGN TO PFMS
        ORGANIZATION IS INDEXED
        ACCESS MODE IS RANDOM
        RECORD KEY IS ITEM-NAME.
*
*
*
DATA DIVISION.
*
FILE SECTION.
*
```

```
 FD  INV-FILE
         RECORD CONTAINS 16 CHARACTERS.
*
 01  INV-RECORD.
     05  ITEM-NAME          PIC X(10).
     05  QUANT-ON-HAND      PIC 999.
     05  REORDER-POINT      PIC 999.
*
*
 WORKING-STORAGE SECTION.
*
 01  DISPLAY-RECORD.
     05  DISP-NAME          PIC X(10).
         88  DONE           VALUE SPACES.
     05  FILLER             PIC X(3) VALUE SPACES.
     05  DISP-QUANT         PIC 999.
     05  FILLER             PIC X(5)   VALUE SPACES.
     05  DISP-REORD         PIC 999.
     05  FILLER             PIC X(5)   VALUE SPACES.
     05  MESSAGE            PIC X(20).
*
 01  POSSIBLE-MESSAGES.
     05  REORD-MSG          PIC X(20) VALUE 'NEEDS
                                        REORDERING'.
     05  BLANK-MSG          PIC X(20) VALUE SPACES.
*
 01  FLAGS.
     05  FOUND-FLAG         PIC XXX.
         88  ITEM-FOUND     VALUE 'YES'.
*
*
*
 PROCEDURE DIVISION.
*
 QUERY-CONTROL.
     PERFORM INITIALIZATION.
     PERFORM GET-NAME.
     PERFORM PROCESS-QUERY
         UNTIL DONE.
     PERFORM WRAP-UP.
     STOP RUN.
*
 INITIALIZATION.
     OPEN INPUT INV-FILE.
     DISPLAY SPACES.
     DISPLAY SPACES.
*
```

```
    GET-NAME.
        DISPLAY 'ENTER NAME OF ITEM TO BE CHECKED'.
        DISPLAY 'PRESS <RETURN> TO EXIT PROGRAM'.
        ACCEPT DISP-NAME.
        DISPLAY SPACES.
        DISPLAY SPACES.
*
    PROCESS-QUERY.
        PERFORM RETRIEVE-RECORD.
        IF   ITEM-FOUND
             THEN PERFORM SHOW-RECORD
             ELSE PERFORM REPORT-ERROR.
        PERFORM GET-NAME.
*
    RETRIEVE-RECORD.
        MOVE 'YES' TO FOUND-FLAG.
        MOVE DISP-NAME TO ITEM-NAME.
        READ INV-FILE
             INVALID KEY MOVE 'NO ' TO FOUND-FLAG.
*
    SHOW-RECORD.
        PERFORM MOVE-FIELDS.
        IF   QUANT-ON-HAND > REORDER-POINT
             THEN MOVE BLANK-MSG TO MESSAGE
             ELSE MOVE REORD-MSG TO MESSAGE.
        DISPLAY DISPLAY-RECORD.
        DISPLAY SPACES.
        DISPLAY SPACES.
        DISPLAY SPACES.
*
    MOVE-FIELDS.
        MOVE ITEM-NAME TO DISP-NAME.
        MOVE QUANT-ON-HAND TO DISP-QUANT.
        MOVE REORDER-POINT TO DISP-REORD.
*
    REPORT-ERROR.
        DISPLAY DISP-NAME, ' IS NOT AN ITEM NAME ON
                                          FILE.'.
        DISPLAY SPACES.
        DISPLAY SPACES.
        DISPLAY SPACES.
*
    WRAP-UP.
        CLOSE INV-FILE.
        DISPLAY 'EXITING PROGRAM'.
        DISPLAY SPACES.
        DISPLAY SPACES.
```

Again, the "bad" example is more efficient than the "good" example: it is shorter, uses fewer variables, and runs more quickly. Both programs work correctly. Which one was easier to understand, and which would be easier to modify?

## CONCLUDING REMARKS

In this chapter we have tried to develop (or review) enough information about good program design and coding to enable students to write acceptable applications programs for file maintenance and retrieval. As suggested in the chapter, there are techniques that have not been discussed (such as validity proofs) because they are beyond the scope of a sophomore-level file processing course. Other courses, such as systems analysis and design or software engineering, would expand on our discussion of these topics, but the presentation here should be adequate for programs assigned at this level.

Over the past few years, we have seen in computer science the emergence of object-oriented programming as an area of interest. A full discussion of this is certainly out of place here, but students should be aware that object-oriented programming is coming and will probably have a significant effect on design and programming issues in the not-too-distant future. Again, it is hoped that the foundations developed in this chapter will be a suitable basis for the adjustments that will be needed in the transition from functional programming to object-oriented programming. Those interested in investigating the area of object-oriented programming should read the series of articles in *BYTE* magazine, or the chapter on object-oriented programming in McLennan's text, both referenced below. The October 1990 issue of *Communications of the ACM* (volume 33, number 9, pages 38–159, eight articles and an introduction) is a special issue devoted to object-oriented design; it is also a good source of information regarding this area.

## EXERCISES

**1.** Explain in your own words each of the characteristics of a good program.

2. In what way (if any) might the order of importance be changed for these characteristics in each of the following five types of programming:

   **(a)** application programs written for in-house use;

   **(b)** software written for commercial sale (such as a spreadsheet package);

   **(c)** software written to support certain hardware (such as a compiler or a printer-control program);

   **(d)** microcode (which consists of instructions written in binary and etched into the circuitry of the CPU to control the execution of all operations of the computer);

   **(e)** real-time systems (in which the execution of the program has to model the current, up-to-the-moment state of affairs, such as the guidance systems for the space shuttle).

3. Explain how you could simulate a selection-control structure in a language that did not have such a construct implemented directly, using conditional and unconditional branching along with statement-line identifiers (such as line numbers).

4. Explain how to simulate test-first iteration using only conditional and unconditional branching.

5. Explain how to simulate test-last iteration.

6. List some of the key differences between the good code and the bad code for the report generation example.

7. Repeat Exercise 6 for the query processing example.

8. Read Dijkstra's letter in the March 1968 issue of *Communications of the ACM.* Do you agree or disagree with his position?

9. Read the letters in the "ACM Forum" sections of the March 1987, May 1987, and June 1987 issues of *Communications of the ACM,* and in the following issues (under "Technical Correspondence") regarding Dijkstra's letter. Do you agree or disagree with them?

10. Look up the original statement of the structure theorem in the May 1966 issue of *Communications of the ACM.* See if you can decipher enough of the article to detect the statement of the theorem given in this chapter.

11. Take a program with several subroutines or procedures and draw the structure chart depicting the organization of the program.

12. Perform a top-down design for the task of managing a printer queue. Allow users to submit files to be printed, to cancel jobs

still waiting, and to display the list of waiting jobs. Allow the "printer" to process the first file in line to be printed.

13. Perform a top-down design for any other programming task of your choice.

14. Perform a top-down design for a nonprogramming task, such as building a bookcase, sewing a dress, or buying a car.

15. Modify each of the Pascal report generating programs so that the items to be reordered appear twenty to a page and double-spaced. (The programs shown would print forty items per page, single-spaced.) What made this modification easier in the "good" example than it was with the "bad" example?

16. Modify the two COBOL query programs so that the difference between the quantity in stock and the reorder point is also displayed, with an indication of the difference being "extra" if the quantity in stock is larger, and "short" if the reorder point is larger. If these two numbers are equal, just print the message that we need to reorder the item. What made this modification easier in the "good" example?

## OTHER READINGS

1. *ACM Computing Surveys,* vol. 6, no. 4 (December 1974). All of these articles deal with programming style.

2. Aron, J. D. *The Program Development Process. Part I: The Individual Programmer* (1974), and *Part II: The Programming Team,* (1983) (Reading, MA: Addison-Wesley).

3. Bohm, Corrado, and Jacopini, Guiseppe. "Flow Diagrams, Turing Machines, and Languages with Only Two Formulation Rules." *Communications of the ACM,* vol. 9, no. 5 (May 1966), p. 366.

4. Brooks, Frederick P., Jr. *The Mythical Man-Month* (Reading, MA: Addison-Wesley, 1975; reprinted with corrections 1982).

5. Cashing, Douglas. "The Role of Structured Programming in Computer Education." *Interface: The Computer Education Quarterly,* vol. 8, issue 3 (Fall 1986), p. 8.

6. *Communications of the ACM,* vol. 33, no. 9 (October 1990).

**7.**   O. Dahl, E. Dijkstra, and C. Hoare. *Structured Programming* (New York: Academic Press, 1972).

**8.**   E. Dijkstra. "GOTO Statements Considered Harmful." *Communications of the ACM,* vol. 11, no. 3 (March 1968), p. 147.

**9.**   Linger, Richard. *Structured Programming: Theory and Practice* (Reading, MA: Addison-Wesley, 1979).

**10.**   MacLennan, Bruce. *Principles of Programming Languages,* 2d ed. (New York: Holt, Rinehart, & Winston, 1987).

**11.**   Miller, George A. "The Magical Number Seven, Plus or Minus Two." *The Psychological Review,* vol. 63, no. 2 (March 1956), p. 81.

**12.**   Parnas, D. L. "On the Criteria To Be Used in Decomposing Systems into Modules." *Communications of the ACM,* vol. 15, no. 12 (December 72), pp. 1053–1058.

**13.**   Tazelaar, Jane (ed.). "In Depth—Object-Oriented Programming." *BYTE,* vol. 14, no. 3 (March 1989), pp. 228–271.

**14.**   Weinberg, Gerald. *Rethinking Systems Analysis and Design* (Boston: Little, Brown, and Co., 1982).

**15.**   Welburn, Tyler. *Advanced Structured COBOL* (Palo Alto, CA: Mayfield/Mitchell, 1983), pp. 2–26.

**16.**   Wirth, Niklaus. "Program Development by Stepwise Refinement." *Communications of the ACM,* vol. 14, no. 4 (April 1971), pp. 221–227.

# 3 MAINTAINING SEQUENTIAL FILES

This chapter will examine the operation of updating a sequentially organized file. We will first consider the layout of the transaction file for a batch updating process, then consider the algorithm for applying that transaction file to the master file. We will conclude the chapter with discussions of backup and recovery of sequential files, creating sequential files, and the most appropriate applications of sequential organization.

## THE NATURE OF THE TRANSACTION FILE

In our study of the process of updating files, we will focus on batch updating in this chapter and in the next two chapters. In batch updating, transaction requests (that is, requests to make changes to the content of the master file) are collected in a transaction file for a period of time, then a program is run that will take each transaction in turn and try to apply it to the master file. This transaction file will usually have a sequential organization, for reasons that we will discuss at the end of this chapter. The format of transaction files described here will be used for updating index-sequential and direct organization files as well.

As we have already seen, there are three types of transactions: adds, changes, and deletions. For our approach, transaction records will have basically the same format as master records, with an update code field appended. Add transactions will contain all the necessary data, in the corresponding fields, for the master record to be created. Change transactions will have the primary key value of the desired master in the transaction key field, and whatever new data are to be put into the master record. These new data will occupy the same positions in the transaction as the old data in the master record. Data fields that are not to be changed will have blank spaces in the corresponding transaction field. (This is referred to as positional change format, as opposed to coded change format, in which the update code for a change has extra information indicating which field to change.) Delete requests must have at least the key value of the record to be deleted. For integrity checking, other data might be included to verify that the record identified by the key value is in fact the one to be dropped. For example, in an employee file keyed to Social Security number, we might include the employee's name in the deletion request. Then when a master record with the same social security number is found, the program will compare names before actually deleting the record. Names that do not match would be considered update errors.

In the transaction file, we must be aware that there might be multiple transactions for the same master record. The proper ordering of these multiple transactions is important. If dates (and times) of submission are kept as part of these transactions, the transactions should probably be completed in order, from earliest to latest. If this information is not available (or if several transactions were submitted on the same date), it is probably reasonable to put add requests first, then changes, and finally deletions. This approach for multiple transactions is most apt to pattern the actual desired updating. Of course, the discussion in this paragraph applies only to transactions for the same master record. Ordering transactions for different master records is a separate issue.

## THE NEED FOR OLD AND NEW MASTER FILES

As we discussed in Chapter 1, records in a sequentially organized file must be accessed sequentially. Also noted in Chapter 1 was the fact that sequential files are normally used either for input or for output, but not for both at the same time. For these reasons, sequentially organized files normally cannot be updated "in place," although some systems are beginning to work around this restriction (allowing both input and output operations to the file in the one program). In view of these considerations, we will use two versions of the master file for updating. The "old" master file is the operational version just prior to the initiation of the update process. The "new" master file will be created during the execution of the update program and will become the desired operational version after the program terminates. At that point, the old master file becomes an archive file. Of course, the file names will need to be changed to distinguish the new master file from the old. Naturally, the record format of the old and new master files will be identical. As we process transactions, we will be using the new master record variables to hold master records that are being modified (or left alone) and to build master records that are being added.

## AN OVERVIEW OF THE ALGORITHM

In considering the algorithm to update a sequential master file, we will assume that the transactions have been validated (and all transactions containing edit errors have been removed from consideration) and are sorted by the value of the master file's primary key (along with whatever ordering has been selected for multiple transactions). The sorting of transactions must be done before the updating process can begin. Validation of all transactions can be done before the sorting is done, which minimizes the number of records to sort but requires two passes through the transaction file; or transactions can be validated during the update process, but this combines the responsibility for two logical operations into one (upper-level) module of the structure chart. Our approach here is to separate the two different logical functions, even though we now have a two-pass operation. This pre-update validation and sorting will be assumed in the next two chapters as well. We will also assume that the master file is in order by primary key values (so steps must have been taken to ensure that records were submitted to the file in key order when the file was created) and that all data in the master file are valid.

The basic approach for our sequential update algorithm is to work through both files at the same time. We start off by opening the files, initializing flags and counters, and reading the first master record and the first transaction record. We now enter a test-first iteration to apply transactions to the master file. Since we are assuming that the transactions are in order by key value, we can now use an algorithm based on comparisons of the transaction key and the master record key. If the values of these two keys are equal, we have found a master record matching the transaction request. We can then process either a change or a deletion, so we invoke the change-or-delete module. If the master key is smaller than the transaction key, then we have processed all transactions for this master record and can now send it to the new master file. If the transaction key is smaller, then there is no matching master record. In this situation, we can process an add request, so the add module is invoked here. This process of comparing keys and selecting an appropriate activity should continue as long as we have transactions and master records to compare. Once the transaction file is exhausted, we can simply transfer all remaining master records over to the new file.

If we run out of master records first, things are a bit more complicated. In the case where transactions are left after the old master file is done, we need to remember that any add requests are valid, as are any changes (or deletions) for these added records. Any other transactions are update errors. What we would like to do is continue using the modules for adds, changes, and deletions that we were using before we ran out of master records. To do this, we need to put an artificially large value into the field holding the master record primary key value. Then any transaction key value will be smaller, triggering the add module. In this way, add requests (and subsequent changes or deletions for the added record) will be processed correctly and other requests will be rejected as update errors. The iteration comparing transaction keys against master keys then continues until the transaction file is exhausted, at which time we move any remaining master records to the new master file. In short, when the master file is exhausted we put an extra-large value in the master key for comparison, tricking the algorithm into thinking that we still have master records to consider.

While this plan will work in theory, we need to realize that the actual primary key field of the master record may have some form of automatic validity checking built in. For example, suppose that a key value may be any three-digit number. The field description in the program for the primary key of the master file might very well be restricted to three-digit integers. Since we may be prevented from placing a value in the key field that is strictly larger than any allowable key value, we could use a temporary copy of the master record key for our comparisons. The description of this temporary key would allow for values larger than the domain of the primary key values of the file. The condition of having exhausted the master file can now be detected by having a super-large value in the temporary master key.

Now we can explain the read modules. When reading the transaction file, all we need to do is set the flag for transaction-end-of-file if the file is exhausted. Depending on the programming language, determining the end-of-file condition may happen before or after the read command is executed. When reading from the old master file, we will need to copy the record found into the program variables for the new master record, since that is where we will be doing all our work. We also need to copy the primary key value into the temporary master key for the comparisons we want to make. If the master file is already exhausted, we need to put a super-high value into the temporary master key in order to continue with the algorithm.

Let us now look at the lower-level modules of the algorithm. The add module was invoked when the transaction key was less than the temporary master key. If the transaction is in fact an add request, we can accomplish the add by building the record to be added in the new master record variables. This overwrites the existing master record that we were not ready to process, so we set the master-pending switch, which tells us that we have a master record (available in the old master record fields) that we will need to retrieve later. If the transaction was not an add request, we have an update error (either a change request or a delete request for a nonexisting master record) that must be reported. In any case, we have processed the transaction record that we had, so we need to read the next transaction record into the program variables. We cannot write the master record to the new file yet because there might be subsequent transactions for this master record.

The pass-master module is invoked when the temporary master key is less than the transaction key. This indicates that all transactions (if any) for this master record have been processed and that this master record is now ready to be sent to the new master file. After writing the master record to the new file, we will need another master record to process. If there was a master record put aside to accommodate an add request, we need to retrieve that pending master record from the old master record variables. Otherwise, we need to read another master record in from the old master file.

The change-or-delete module would be invoked when the two key values are equal. If the request is for a change, the algorithm will move any nonblank fields from the transaction record into the corresponding fields of the new master record (except for the primary key, which already has the correct value). If the request is for a deletion, it is sufficient to get another master record to process, since this will overwrite the program variables without sending the data to the new file. If the transaction is an add request, then we have encountered an update error (duplicating a primary key value). In any case, the current transaction has been processed and we are ready for the next one.

The last consideration here is finishing the master file, which is done after all transactions are processed and is controlled by a test-first iteration if there are master records left. The task is to write the data currently in the new master record variables to the new file, then try to get another master record to send along.

We conclude this section with two comments. First, notice that the iteration to process a record does not read that record. The record being processed was read before that pass through the iteration. Notice also that the last operation of the pass is to read the record to be processed on the next pass through the iteration. This is called a read-ahead scheme, and will be used frequently in this book. Second, notice that the specifics of this algorithm (which will be presented in the next section) will need to be modified in some places to fit the grammar of the programming language to be used for implementation. The one main example of this is the issue of reading from a file when we might have already reached the end of the file. Some languages allow you to check for this condition before a read command is issued (and will crash if you read anyway). Other languages require the read command to be given in order to determine if the end of the file has been reached. We will use the first form in the pseudocode, realizing that it may need to be modified in program code.

## THE ALGORITHM IN DETAIL

The algorithm presented here is one approach to updating a sequentially organized master file in batch mode. The justification and explanation of these modules was given in the previous section. Recall that we are assuming that the transactions have been validated and that all transactions containing edit errors have been reported and removed from consideration. This might be done with a completely separate program or as a first stage of the update program. The algorithm here does not include any of the mechanics for formatting the update error report, for reporting audits, or for keeping any summary tallies, since these depend very heavily on the user's requirements. Again, notice that the two iteration structures in the main-level module are both test-first.

### Update the Sequential Master File

```
initialize the variables and open the files
Read-master
Read-transaction
until the end of the transaction file is reached
      Do-updating
until temporary master key = super-high value
      Pass-master
print the summary tallies and close the files
terminate the run
```

### Read–master

```
if   the old master file has been exhausted
then put a super-high value into the temporary
                                    master key
     set the end-of-master-flag
else read the next record into the old master
                                   record area
     copy the old master record into the new
                                 master record
     copy the new master key into the temporary
                                    master key
```

### Read-transaction

```
if   the transaction file is exhausted
then set the end-of-trans-flag
else read the next transaction record
```

### Do-updating

```
if   trans key is smaller than temp master key
then Assume-add
else if  temp master key is smaller than trans
                                            key
         then  Pass-master
         else  Assume-change-or-delete
```

### Assume–add

```
if   the transaction is an add request
then set the master-pending switch
     load data into new master record fields
     copy transaction key to temp master key
else report an update error
Read-transaction
```

### Pass–master

```
write the new master record data to the new file
if   there is a master pending
then Retrieve-master
else Read-master
```

### Assume–change–or–delete

```
if   the transaction is a change request
then Modify-master
else if    the transaction is a delete request
     then   Drop-master
     else   report an update error
Read-transaction
```

### Retrieve–master

```
if   the old master file has been exhausted
then put super-high value in temp master key
else copy old master record to new master record
     copy new master key to temporary master key
     turn off the master-pending switch
```

### Modify–master

```
copy nonblank transaction fields to the new
                                    master record
{except for the primary key value}
```

### Drop–master

```
if   there is a master record pending
then Retrieve-master
else Read-master
```

## CHANGING THE PRIMARY KEY VALUE

Normally, once a record has been assigned its primary key value, there should be no reason to change it unless there has been a data-entry error when the record was added to the file (as when the key value that was typed in was not the value intended). If such a data-entry error occurs, the existing record must be deleted and the correct version submitted as an add request. In this process, steps must be taken to preserve the data in the record for use in the add.

## BACKING UP AND CREATING SEQUENTIAL FILES

Since storing a sequential file requires a minimal amount of system overhead, making a backup is very simple. All computer systems should have a command for making an exact duplicate of a file, which is all that is needed here. With a recent backup file available, this same duplicate command can be used to recover the operational file if it is accidentally lost or damaged. Normally, the backup file should be put on a different secondary storage device from the operational version of the file.

Creating a sequential file is also straightforward, although there are several options as to how to proceed here. One approach is to use a text editor or word processing package to enter the original data into the newly created file, which puts the burden of validating and sequencing the data on the data-entry person. Another approach is to write a special one-time file creation program, perhaps using the text editor file mentioned above as input. This program would check each master record for validity, then sort all the master records into proper order before sending them to the newly created master file. A variation on this is the use of a data loading utility package, if your system has such a feature. The final alternative is to create an empty master file, create a transaction file with add requests for the original data, and run the updating program(s) to validate and sort the transactions, then apply them to the master file.

## WHEN TO USE SEQUENTIAL ORGANIZATION

Naturally, the organization must be selected before the file is created and cannot be changed during the file's existence. If the selected organization proves to be unsuitable for the desired processing, a new file with the proper organization must be created and the data from the old file must be transferred over to the new version.

Basically, sequential organization works very well when most of the processing activities will use most of the records in the file. We have focused on updating in this chapter, but there are other processing activities (such as report generation or query processing) that will need to be done. If we are going to want to access most (or all) of the records in most of our processing, an organization that requires us to access records in order from the beginning is not a drawback and we will not be encumbered by system overhead that we don't really need. Sequential organization works very well for such processing as checking all items in an inventory file for possible reordering, but it is not suitable for the task of getting the amount in stock for a particular item requested by a customer.

## CONCLUDING REMARKS

Now that we have looked at an approach to updating sequentially organized files, a few summary comments are probably in order. We have observed the need for two versions of the master file, one pre-update and the other post-update, since sequential files usually cannot be updated in place. This also requires the update algorithm to be very careful about when to write (and when not to write) the master records. In the next two chapters, we will see that files that can provide random access are not affected by these issues.

The update algorithm given here is just one of several that could be used. Other approaches are referenced below. In Chapter 9, particularly in the section on merging, you should notice a similarity to the updating algorithm presented here, since in a very real sense this approach "merges" the transactions into the master file. Chapter 9 could easily be studied next as a continuation of sequential file operations, or you could continue to follow updating procedures through the various file organizations instead. At this point, either choice would be quite reasonable.

## EXERCISES

**1.** Draw the structure chart for the algorithm given here.

**2.** Explain the role of the master-pending switch in the algorithm.

3. Explain why the new master records are not written to the new file more frequently in the algorithm.

4. Explain the role of the super-high key value mentioned in the algorithm.

5. What would be some of the potential problems if the transaction records were not sorted by primary key value before running the update procedure?

6. There are six possible orderings for multiple transactions. The one suggested here was adds-changes-deletions. What are the other five? What update errors would occur in each ordering if the key value is already in the file? What update errors would occur if the key value is not in the file?

7. What are the benefits of incorporating validation in the update process? What are the benefits of doing the validation first, as a process separate from updating?

8. Give some examples of data files and processing tasks for which sequential organization would be suitable. Give some examples where it wouldn't be.

9. What are the advantages and disadvantages of positional change format as opposed to coded change format?

10. Why is sequential organization normally used for the transaction file?

11. Compare the sequential update algorithm in Dwyer's article (identified as Figure 4 in the article) with the one given here. Which do you think is preferable, and why?

12. Develop an algorithm based on transaction type rather than key comparisons. Is this a better or worse algorithm than the one given here, and why?

---

## PROGRAMMING PROJECT

Write a program to implement the algorithm given here for updating a sequentially organized file. Your instructor will provide the details regarding the layout of the master file and its records, formatting for the update error report (as well as the edit error and audit reports, if any), and desired summary totals (if any). Be sure your program can handle multiple transactions and will operate correctly regardless of which input file is exhausted first.

## OTHER READINGS

**1.** Dwyer, Barry. "One More Time—How to Update a Master File," *Communications of the ACM,* vol. 24, no. 1 (January 1981), pp. 3–8.

**2.** Miller, Nancy. *File Structures Using Pascal* (Menlo Park, CA: Benjamin Cummings, 1987), Chapter 5.

**3.** Welburn, Tyler. *Advanced Structured COBOL* (Palo Alto, CA: Mayfield/Mitchell, 1983), Chapter 3.

# 4 MAINTAINING DIRECT ORGANIZATION FILES

In this chapter, we will examine the direct organization file structure in more detail. We start with a review of direct organization and its four variant forms and then consider an algorithm for updating direct organization files with direct addressing. After that we will review the linked data structures that we will need for updating direct organization files with indirect addressing and consider the algorithm for updating such files. The issues of backing up and creating these files will be discussed, along with considerations of when they are most appropriately used. We will conclude with an overview of considerations for performance analysis of hashing and a brief discussion of some more exotic variations of hashing.

## A REVIEW OF DIRECT ORGANIZATION

Recall from Chapter 1 that in direct organization each record key corresponds to a location in the file where the record belongs. What we mean by location and the nature of the key-to-location correspondence determine the four variations of direct organization: (1) actual-direct, (2) actual-indirect, (3) relative-direct, and (4) relative-indirect. The ordering of records in the file does not have to be the same as the order of the key values and may appear to be random, which is why these files are sometimes called random files.

### Actual Addressing

Actual addressing is used in the actual-direct and the actual-indirect variations. Location is based on the physical machine address. This approach is not viable at the application programming or software package levels because the operating system is involved in file access and the file location is apt to change every time the disk is reorganized (which should be done periodically on any reasonably active system). Actual addressing is, of course, the manner in which the operating system's file manager must eventually work, since the actual retrieval at the machine level must be done in terms of the physical machine address.

## Relative Addressing

The alternative to actual addressing is relative addressing, used in the relative-direct and the relative-indirect variations, in which each location (or record slot) is referred to by its position in the file relative to the other slots. Thus, the first slot is location number 1, the second is number 2, and so on (on some systems, the numbering starts with 0 instead of 1). Since this is the form used at the application programming and software package levels, we will concentrate on relative addressing in this chapter.

## Direct Addressing

The correspondence between key value and desired location also has two options. In direct addressing, which is used in the actual-direct and the relative-direct variations (and should not be confused with direct organization), the key value is the desired location. This simplifies the programming associated with the file but it can be very wasteful of space. For example, at St. Bonaventure University we use a seven-digit student identification number. This allows us to uniquely identify all students, past, present, and future. If we were to use these identification numbers as the primary keys for the student data records under direct addressing, we would need 10,000,000 record slots (if we use slot numbers from 0 to 9,999,999) to ensure that each legitimate identification number had a corresponding location. Because we have at most 3,000 active students, only 0.03 percent of the file space would be in use. (Recall that direct organization usually requires that all record slots be established when the file is created.)

## Indirect Addressing

To avoid this problem and conserve space, we can use indirect addressing, or hashing, to compute a location from the key value. Indirect addressing is used in actual-indirect and relative-indirect organization. Hashing is also necessary if the key values are not acceptable location values (such as nonnumeric keys or numeric keys in a range that is different from the range of location values).

There are many standard hashing schemes available and variations can be concocted as needed by individual users. The one that seems to be useful most often, however, is the prime division/remainder scheme. In this hash function, the (numeric) key value of the record is divided by the appropriate prime number. The integer remainder of this division (or perhaps the remainder plus one) is taken as the desired location, or home address, for the record. The best prime number to use is the largest prime that is no larger than the number of home locations allocated for the file.

Usually, hashing functions are not one-to-one, meaning that many different key values will hash to the same location number. As you will recall, these keys are called synonyms, and trying to include more than one of them in the file is called a collision. Any indirect addressing scheme must include a method of handling these collisions. One approach is progressive overflow, in which each colliding record is stored in the next available location. This is probably the easiest overflow scheme to understand, but is probably the least efficient for retrieval operations. The other scheme that we will consider here is chained overflow. In this approach, each home address is the first node of a linked list. The other nodes, if any, are slots in a logically separate overflow area that holds records whose keys are synonyms of the key value in the home slot. This linked structure is more complicated to visualize at first, but it allows more efficient processing and becomes understandable with practice. The use of chained overflow, as will be explained later in the chapter, will provide a better understanding of direct organization files and will be a good review of the linked data structures.

## DIRECT ADDRESSING: AN OVERVIEW OF THE UPDATE ALGORITHM

Because direct organization files can be used for both input and output in the same program, we do not need to have two versions of the master file. Rather, we can update the master file "in place," reading records into the program, modifying them, and rewriting them to the file as needed. Since direct organization files also support random access, we don't need to hold a master record until all transactions for it are processed (as we did when updating sequential files). If there are multiple transactions for a master record, we can retrieve it repeatedly from the master, operate on it, and rewrite it back to the master file. Thus, the sorting of transactions is not essential to the updating process. However, the order in which multiple updates are applied to the file can only be controlled by sorting the transactions, so we will assume that this has been done before the update algorithm is applied.

As in Chapter 3, we will also want to have validated the transactions before the update algorithm begins. In the algorithm we will assume that the contents of a record slot must be read into the corresponding program variables in order to perform a rewrite operation to it. (This is not required on all systems, but it is probably a good idea anyway.) The algorithm also assumes that all record slots had to be allocated and initialized when the file was created. Thus, all output operations to the file are rewrites that replace the contents of a slot rather than create a new slot. In other words, every slot exists and has something in it, although it may not necessarily contain an actual data record.

The algorithm will work through the transaction file and attempt to process each transaction in turn until that file is exhausted. Using a read-ahead scheme (where we read the first transaction outside the loop, process the transaction in the loop, and read the next transaction at the bottom of the loop), we iterate, applying one transaction per pass to the master file, until all transactions are handled.

As each transaction is read into the program variables, the algorithm will take its primary key value, copy it into the relative key field (which the system uses as the slot number to access), and retrieve that record slot from the file. (Please note that the nature of this step is apt to be system-dependent. The manner in which your system and/or programming language handles this may vary from the algorithm here.) If the master record has actual data in it, the primary key field of the master record will match the transaction key and we will set a master-found flag. If the slot does not contain actual data, its key field will contain a special "not-in-use" value and we will turn off the master-found flag.

Inside the loop, we call one of three modules, depending on the type of transaction we have (add, change, or delete). For a change request, if the master is found, we move the new data into the appropriate fields and rewrite the record to the master file. Of course, if the master record is not found, we report an update error.

For an add request, if a matching master is found we have an update error. Otherwise, we load the data from the transaction record fields into the master record fields and rewrite the record.

For a deletion, we again report an update error if no matching master record is found. Otherwise, we "blank out" the master record variables and rewrite the record.

---

## DIRECT ADDRESSING: THE ALGORITHM IN DETAIL

### *Apply Transactions*

```
Initialize
Read Trans
until eof-trans
     Do Update
Wrap Up
terminate the program
```

### *Initialize*

```
open the files
initialize the flags and counters
```

### *Read Trans*

```
if   not end-of-transactions
then read a transaction record
     copy transaction key to relative key
     Read Master Record
else set eof-trans
```

### *Read Master Record*

```
read from the master file
if    Master-Key = Transaction-Key
then  turn on Master-Found flag
else  turn off Master-Found Flag
```

### Do Update

```
if    Add-Request
then  Attempt Add
else  if    Change-Request
      then  Attempt Change
      else  Attempt Delete
Read Trans
```

### Attempt Add

```
if    Master-Found
then  report update error
else  copy trans data into master record fields
      rewrite the master record
```

### Attempt Change

```
if    Master-Found
then  move nonblank trans fields to master fields
      rewrite the master record
else  report update error
```

### Attempt Delete

```
If    not Master-Found
then  report update error
else  put "not-in-use" key value into primary
                                    key field

      "blank out" other fields
      rewrite the master record
```

### Wrap Up

```
print summary totals
close the files
```

## A REVIEW OF LINKED LISTS, STACKS, AND QUEUES

In this section we will take a quick look at the three basic linked data structures. The presentation here assumes that these structures have been studied before, so the discussion is not as extensive as it would be for a first exposure to these concepts.

## Linked Lists

In any linked structure, we deal with nodes. Each node has a data area for storing information and one or more linking areas for connecting nodes together. There will be one or more external "links" used to gain initial access to the structure. Once we have accessed the structure, we can use the linking area(s) of the current node to move through the structure, examining and using data as we go. The nature of these linking areas depends on the implementation used. In languages that provide dynamic allocation (where storage space for variables is set up as needed during execution of the program), we can use the language's "pointer" data type for the internal and external links. In languages with static allocation (where space for the variables must be allocated before execution time), we must use arrays to implement the linked structures. In this case, each link will be an index into the array structure. Since the implementation does not affect the logic of the linked data structures, we will not worry about it any further at this point.

The different linked structures are distinguished by the internal relationship of the nodes within the structure and by how these nodes are supposed to be accessed by the user. In a simple linked list, the nodes are viewed as being arranged in a linear fashion. There is one external pointer, usually referred to as FIRST, that identifies the first node in the list. Each node is linked to the next node in order, and the last is not linked to anything, or, more precisely, has a "null" value in its link field. The user may access the first node in the list via FIRST, and then may access each node in turn via the link area of the currently accessed node, until the last node of the list has been reached. Any node in the list is thus available to the user to examine, modify, or delete. New data nodes may be inserted into the list at the appropriate location, whether at the beginning, in the middle, or at the end of the list. The decision as to where a node belongs depends on the nature of the ordering desired for that data set. This data structure is useful when alphabetizing or in other situations where one wants to keep data in an order that is not based on arrival time. It is also useful if one needs full access to all the data items in the structure.

The two main variants of the standard linear linked list are the circular linked list, in which the last node points back to the first node instead of being null, and the two-way list, where each node has two link fields, one to the node following it and the other to the node preceding it.

Let us quickly review the algorithms for insertion and deletion of data nodes when working with a simple linear linked list. In these algorithms, all variables are taken as global. The variables FIRST, TEMP, PREVIOUS, CURRENT, and NEW are of the data type used for links (whatever that type actually is in the language of implementation). The insertion algorithm does not check the requested data for duplication of data already in the list.

To delete a data node from a linked list:

```
if     FIRST is null
then   report error
else   access FIRST node
if     data matches delete request
then   Remove_First
else   Find_Node
       if    node is found
       then  Remove_Node
       else  report error

Remove_First:
    TEMP <<-- FIRST
    FIRST <<-- FIRST's link
    dispose or reformat TEMP by appropriate
                                      command(s)

Find_Node:
    PREVIOUS <<-- FIRST
    CURRENT <<-- FIRST's link
    while (CURRENT not null) and (node not found)
        if   data in CURRENT is not delete request
        then PREVIOUS <<-- CURRENT
             CURRENT <<-- CURRENT's pointer
        else node is found

Remove_Node:
    PREVIOUS's link <<-- CURRENT's link
    dispose or reformat CURRENT by appropriate
                                      command(s)
```

To insert a new data node (without checking for duplication):

```
*** If there is space in the structure ***

create or find an unused node NEW by the proper
                                     command(s)
load data into data part of NEW
if    FIRST is null
then  FIRST <<-- NEW
      NEW's link <<-- null
else  if    NEW belongs before FIRST
      then  Insert_First
      else  Find_Spot
            Insert_Node

Insert_First:
    NEW's link <<-- FIRST
    FIRST <<-- NEW

Find_Spot:
    PREVIOUS <<-- FIRST
    CURRENT <<-- FIRST's link
    while (spot not found) and (CURRENT not null)
        if    NEW belongs before CURRENT
        then  spot is found
        else  PREVIOUS <<-- CURRENT
              CURRENT <<-- CURRENT's link

Insert_Node:
    PREVIOUS's link <<-- NEW
    NEW's link <<-- CURRENT
```

## Stacks

A stack is quite similar to a simple linear linked list in its organization. The main difference is that the user is only supposed to have access to the first node in the structure (usually referred to as TOP). The user may add new nodes to the stack, but only by pushing them onto the top of the stack (i.e., by adding them in front of all existing nodes). The user may delete (or pop) the top node from the stack. Any node other than the one on top is assumed to be inaccessible to the user, at least until all nodes before it have been removed from the stack. This structure is very useful for dealing with data that must be processed in the reverse order from which it was received (last in-first out), as in keeping track of nested procedure calls during program execution.

Let us now examine the algorithms for pushing and popping. Again, variables are global and of the same type as the link field.

To push new data onto the stack:

```
*** If there is space in the structure ***
create or find an unused node NEW by the proper
                                        command(s)
load the data into NEW's data area
NEW's link <<-- TOP
TOP <<-- NEW
```

To pop data from the stack:

```
if    TOP is null
then  report error
else  process TOP's data as required
      TEMP <<-- TOP
      TOP <<-- TOP's link
      dispose or reformat TEMP by the
                        appropriate command(s)
```

## Queues

A queue is also similar to a linked list in organization, but it has two external pointers, one to the first node (called FRONT) and one to the last (called BACK). We are allowed to process and remove the FRONT node of the queue and we are allowed to append new nodes following BACK. We are not to have access to nodes other than the one in FRONT. Queues provide a good structure for data that are to be processed in the order that it is received (first in-first out), as when handling files sent to a printer. As with linked lists and stacks, the algorithms for inserting and deleting are given here.

To add a node to the queue:

```
*** If there is space in the structure ***

create or find an unused node NEW using the
                            proper command(s)
load the data into NEW's data area
put the null value into New's link field
if    BACK is null (when the queue is empty)
then  FRONT <<-- NEW
      BACK <<-- NEW
else  BACK's link <<-- NEW
      BACK <<-- NEW
```

To remove a node from the queue:

```
if     FRONT is null
then   report an error
else   process the data from FRONT as required
       TEMP <<-- FRONT
       FRONT <<-- FRONT's link
       dispose or reformat TEMP by the
                           appropriate command(s)
       if    FRONT is null
       then  BACK <<-- null
```

# IMPLEMENTING CHAINED OVERFLOW WITH STATIC ALLOCATION

Normally, all record slots to be used in a direct organization file must be allocated when the file is created. This means that we have static allocation of a predetermined number of slots. If we are using indirect addressing with chained overflow, the chains of overflow records, and the available overflow slots, must be implemented with the array-type structures mentioned above. In particular, the overflow area must be maintained in such a way as to keep track of each of the overflow chains and to keep track of the overflow slots that are not in use at any given time. Thus, we need a data structure for the overflow chains and a data structure for the free space, and we must implement these structures under static allocation.

The structure for the overflow chains should be a linked list, since we may need to access any record in the chain. This will allow us to process, modify, or delete any record as needed. It would also allow us to insert new records into the chain at any point, but unless there is a real need to order the records by some data value, the best approach is to add new records at the end of the appropriate chain. This is the approach that will be used in our algorithm.

The choice of structure to use for the free space may be less obvious. Notice, however, that any free slot is as good as any other, so the logic of the situation does not favor any structure over any other. We should then pick the simplest structure to manipulate, which would be the stack. We will take advantage of this relative simplicity in our file structure.

At the time the file is created and before data are loaded, all slots in the overflow area are available. Thus, each of these slots should be in the stack of free space. The top pointer will indicate which slot to use first when we get a collision, and each slot in the stack will indicate which slot to use next. The last slot in the stack will have the null pointer, letting us know at that point that there are no more overflow slots available. As colliding data records are loaded into the file, or as they are added to the file later on, we will "pop" the top slot from the stack of free space and use it for the new record. In doing this, we need to be sure that there is a slot available in the stack. Otherwise, we have an update error specific to direct organization files, namely "file full—can't add." If an overflow slot is available, we'll load the new data into the slot, set its pointer to null, and connect it to the end of the linked list that started at the record's home address. When a record in an overflow slot is deleted, we will remove the data from the slot and "push" that slot onto the top of the stack. We also have to reconnect the linked list from which the record was deleted.

The first node in each linked list is the home address for the records in the list. This address (which then plays the role of FIRST in the algorithms above), is computed by the hashing function chosen for this file. Thus, we don't need to worry about saving the value of these external pointers—the value will be computed as needed. The external pointer for the stack of free space, however, must be saved with the file, since there is no way of computing it. The simplest approach is to store this pointer value in a special record slot in the file. Then the update program can access this slot when the file is opened, read the pointer value into its TOP variable, and process the file correctly. Of course, if TOP changes during execution, the program must put this new value back into the slot that holds it before closing the file.

## INDIRECT ADDRESSING: AN OVERVIEW OF THE UPDATE ALGORITHM

In the update algorithm for indirect addressing, we will assume that the transactions have been validated and sorted before the update algorithm begins and we will not be concerned with holding a master record until all transactions for it are processed, just as in the algorithm for direct addressing. The main iteration and the read-ahead scheme are also the same.

This time, however, as a transaction is read into the program variables, the algorithm will check for a matching master record. This is done by computing (and saving) the home address, reading the home address slot into the program variables, and comparing the key fields of the transaction and the master record. A master-found flag will be set according to the result of this comparison. We will also set a home-open flag, indicating whether this home slot contains a data record or is unused at present. If necessary, the algorithm will then search through the linked list of overflow records connected to this home address for a matching record, keeping track of the current and previous nodes as it goes along. When this process is complete, the program "knows" whether a matching master record was found. If there is a matching master record, the program will "know" where that record is and what record immediately precedes it in the chain. If no match exists, the program "knows" where the end of the chain is.

Inside the loop, we again call the appropriate module, depending on the type of transaction we have (add, change, or delete). For a change request, if the master is found, we move the new data into the appropriate fields and rewrite the record to the master file. Of course, if the master record is not found, we report an update error.

For an add request, if a matching master is found we have an update error. Otherwise, we need to determine whether the new record belongs in the home slot or in overflow. Hence, the home-open switch is used to call the proper module for the actual add. If the home slot is open, we merely load the data for the new record into the program variables and rewrite the record to the master file. If the home slot is already in use, we have a collision and must use an overflow slot to store the new record. If there is an available slot, we pop it off the stack, load the data into it, set the link to null, rewrite it to the file, read the slot that used to be the end of this overflow chain, set its link to the slot we just used for the new record, and rewrite it to the file. However, if there are no available overflow slots, which can happen with static allocation, we have to report an update error and reject the add request. Remember that this file-full condition will be indicated by the top-of-stack pointer being null.

For a deletion, we again report an update error if no matching master record is found. Otherwise, we decide whether we are deleting the contents of a home slot or an overflow slot and call the appropriate module to execute the deletion. If we are deleting an overflow slot, we save the record's link, blank out the record and push it onto the stack of free space, read the slot just before the deleted slot in the chain, reset its link, and rewrite it to the file. If we are deleting a record stored in a home slot, we need to be concerned with any overflow chain connected to it. If there is no chain, we merely blank out the record and rewrite it. If there is a chain of overflow records connected to this home slot, we will move the first overflow record into the home position. This is done by reading the first overflow slot into the program variables and copying it to a temporary record area for later use. We then read the home slot again, move the data from the temporary area into the master record variables (overwriting the record to be deleted), and rewrite the record to the master file. We then go back to the first overflow slot (whose data now appear twice in the file) and delete it as before (except that the link in the previous record is already correct and so does not need to be reset).

Again, we need to remember to access the top-of-stack pointer from the file as part of the initialization process and to store this pointer back into the file after the updating is finished but before the program terminates. While it may not appear so at first, the algorithm here is basically the same as the one we used for updating a direct-address file.

## INDIRECT ADDRESSING: THE ALGORITHM IN DETAIL

Address variables:

*1.* Top-Holder: address of the slot that stores the top-of-stack pointer between runs of the update program

*2.* Top: the address of the first available overflow slot

*3.* Relative-Key: the number of the slot that will be accessed by the system on an I/O operation

*4.* Current: the slot number currently being examined

*5.* Previous: the number of the slot just before Current in the chain of overflow records

*6.* Next: the number of the slot belonging just after Current

*7.* Link: the value in the link field of the record in the program variables

### Apply Transactions

```
Initialize
Read Trans
until eof-trans
     Do Update
Wrap Up
terminate the program
```

## *Initialize*

```
open the files
initialize the flags and counters
put Top-Holder into Relative-Key
read from the master file
put Link into Top
```

## *Read Trans*

```
if     not the end of the transaction file
then   read a transaction record
       Compute Home Address
       Search For Master
```

## *Compute Home*

```
apply the hashing scheme to the transaction key
store the result in Home-Address and in Current
```

## *Search For Master*

```
put Home-Address into Relative-Key
Read Master File
if     master key has the value of an unused slot
then   turn on the Home-Open flag
else   turn off the Home-Open flag

until  Master-Found or Link is null
       put Relative-Key into Previous
       put Link into Current
       put Current into Relative-Key
       Read Master File
```

## *Read Master File*

```
read from the master file
if     Master-Key = Transaction-Key
then   turn on Master-Found flag
else   turn off Master-Found flag
```

### Do Update

```
If     Add-Request
then   Attempt Add
else   if    Change-Request
       then  Attempt Change
       else  Attempt Delete
Read Trans
```

### Attempt Add

```
if     Master-Found
then   report update error
else   if    Home-Open
       then  Add Home
       else  Add Overflow
```

### Add Home

```
load the data into the master record variables
set Link to null
rewrite the master record
```

### Add Overflow

```
Get Overflow Slot
if     Space-Available
then   load the data into the program variables
       set Link to null
       rewrite the master record
       put Current into Relative-Key
       read from the master file
       put New into Link
       rewrite the master record
else   report update error [file full--can't
                                     add]
```

### Get Overflow Slot

```
if     Top is null
then   turn off Space-Available flag
else   turn on Space-Available flag
       put Top into New
       put New into Relative-Key
       read from the master file
       put Link into Top
```

### Attempt Change

```
if    Master-Found
then  move non-blank trans fields to master
                                          fields
      rewrite the master record
else  report update error
```

### Attempt Delete

```
if    not Master-Found
then  report update error
else  if    Current = Home-Address
      then  Delete Home
      else  Delete Overflow
```

### Delete Home

```
if    Link is null
then  Reformat Record
      put null into Link
      rewrite the master record
else  put Link into Current
      put Current into Relative-Key
      read from the master file
      copy Master-Record to Temp-Record
      put Home-Address into Relative-Key
      read from the master file
      copy Temp-Record to Master-Record
      rewrite the master record
      put Current into Relative-Key
      read from the master file
      Return To Stack
```

### Delete Overflow

```
put Link into Next
Return To Stack
Reconnect List
```

### Return To Stack

```
Reformat Record
put Top into Link
rewrite the master record
put Current into Top
```

### Reconnect List

```
put Previous into Relative-Key
read from the master file
put Next into Link
rewrite the master record
```

### Reformat Record

```
put key value of unused slots into key field
put spaces in all other data fields
```

### Wrap Up

```
put Top-Holder into Relative-Key
read from the master file
put Top into Link
rewrite the master record
print summary totals
close the files
```

## BACKING UP AND CREATING DIRECT ORGANIZATION FILES

In backing up a file, the main objective is to make a copy of the data that can be stored in a separate location in case of damage to the operational file. The internal structure of the file does not need to be copied, so normally we do not want to use the system's COPY command to back up our direct organization file. This would duplicate the data as desired, but it would also duplicate all of the associated overhead that the system needs. To copy the data without recreating this overhead, we can write a small conversion program that will read each record in turn from the direct organization data file and write it to a sequentially organized backup file. Of course, this requires a restoration program that can read from the sequential backup and write to a recreated version of the operational file. In those computer systems that offer utilities to accomplish this conversion-backup-restoration procedure, writing these application programs is not necessary. In most systems, this conversion to sequential organization is also needed in order to print a hard copy of the data file for examination, although such printouts would rarely be needed in normal usage.

Creating a direct organization file is also different from the creation process discussed in the last chapter. Generally, we will need to first create a template for the file through a system utility. This template will be based on information from the file's creator regarding such things as the size and nature of the primary key, the length of each record, and the number of record slots to allocate. This process allows the system to set up the internal structuring for both the data file and its structure for access overhead. Once this template has been created, we can load the first set of data into the file, which can be done through a system utility (if one exists and offers the level of validity checking we need) or by means of an application program. Such a program would consist essentially of the restoration program mentioned above, augmented by the required validity checking.

## WHEN TO USE DIRECT ORGANIZATION

Direct organization is preferred when we need the ability to randomly access records and when the speed of retrieval is more important than the complexity of the programming. Recall that index-sequential organization will also allow random access, but because of its implementation the retrieval of a given record will be slower. On the other hand, it is much simpler to program for access of an index-sequential file than for a direct organization file. Two observations should be made here. First, the faster retrieval speed of direct organization assumes that the program already "knows" which record slot is needed. If an overflow chain of any length needs to be searched for the desired record, the retrieval could actually be slower because of the multiple fetches. Second, although direct organization is faster, its advantage over index-sequential is not as great as it once was. Improvements in hardware and operating systems have decreased the difference between the retrieval times for these two organizations.

We should also note here that some programming environments do not support index-sequential organization. In such situations, we will be forced to use some form of direct organization to provide random access to records in the file, whether we are concerned with the speed of retrieval or not.

## PERFORMANCE ANALYSIS OF HASHING FUNCTIONS

One of the most important factors in designing a direct organization file with indirect addressing is the selection of a "good" hashing function. If one is really concerned with the performance of retrieval programs using this file, the choice of hashing function will require a long and careful analysis of record placement in the file. The main objective is to minimize the average search length. Search length is defined as the number of reads to the file needed to obtain the desired record. For example, if the record we want is the third overflow record in a chain, the search length is 4 (one for the home address, and one for each of the three overflow slots that had to be accessed). The average of these search lengths for each record in the file is the usual measure of the quality of the hashing function. The operational rule of thumb seems to be that an average search length of 2 or more is unacceptable. An average of 1.5 or less is considered reasonable. Search lengths of between 1.5 and 2 are not really very good, but might be considered tolerable.

We should note here that we have suddenly made a change from concentrating on design issues (such as how many records we might need to have and how long the records are) to concern over the actual data values we believe we will get in the file. One does not need to know what primary key values will actually occur in the file to decide how many record slots to provide, but one must know the primary key values existing in the file to compute the average search length. Since these key values will change over time as insertions and deletions are made, a hashing function that was quite good when the file was created may be rather poor after a period of time has elapsed. Unfortunately, changing the hashing function requires the creation of a whole new file and the transfer of the data from the old file to the new one. Thus, at the time the file is created, the design team should focus on the best description of typical key value distributions, and not just look at the initial set of data for the file. Average search length for a "typical" sample should be computed for each hashing function under consideration until an acceptable one is found.

In addition to the choice of hashing function, there are two other design issues that will affect the average search length. The first is the number of home addresses provided. We would certainly expect that increasing the number of possible addresses to which we can hash would reduce the number of collisions and hence the number of overflow records encountered. Of course, any parameters in the hashing function (such as the prime number by which to divide in the prime division/remainder hashing function) would have to be changed accordingly in order to take advantage of these additional slots.

The other factor to be considered is the number of records that can be stored at an address. Up to this point we have been assuming that one slot will hold one record. However, if we double the size of each slot, one address could hold two records. A read operation will retrieve the contents of the designated slot and bring two records into the program variables. The program code would then have to deal with the two records separately in the operations. Notice, however, that we are now able to have two records per home address with no overflow, which cuts the search length of overflow records by about half. Of course, the search length of home records will still be 1. Depending on the length of each record and the size of the transfer buffer (which will be considered in Chapter 7), we might consider address capacities of three, four, or five records per address. As typically happens in this sort of situation, the gain in retrieval time from increased slot capacity needs to be balanced against the increased programming complexity required to separate the records inside the program code.

In examining hashing functions and considering the number of home addresses and slot capacity, we have been striving to reduce the average search length. The ultimate goal is what is usually referred to as uniform distribution of records, where each home address receives the same number of records under the hashing as every other home address. Of course, if the number of slots does not evenly divide the number of records, there will be some slots that have one more record than other slots. Even so, in distributing records so that no two slots differ by more than one record, we have a hashing function that minimizes the average search length. Any further reductions will have to come by adding more home addresses (which may reduce the effectiveness of the hashing function) or by increasing slot capacity. Ideally, we would have this uniform record distribution along with enough home addresses to accommodate all of the records. For example, with one record per slot and 1,000 records to store, we would want uniform distribution and at least 1,000 slots. If slot capacity were three records per slot, we would want at least 334 home addresses for the 1,000 records (along with uniform distribution). This would give us an average search length of 1, which is optimal.

Of course, a uniform distribution of records is very hard to achieve unless the primary key values themselves have a characteristic pattern that can be exploited in selecting a hashing function. At the other end of consideration is random distribution of records, in which any home address is as likely as any other to be used for each added record, without regard for the number of records that have already been hashed to that home address. This is considered a poor situation, since the average search length can be expected to be 2 by the time 65 percent of the slots have been filled. So, while we can't expect our hashing functions to necessarily produce uniform record distribution, we would certainly want them to do better than random record distribution. The full analysis of what to actually expect under random distribution of records requires more in the way of probability theory than we will cover here, but we can note that this analysis involves a determination of how many home addresses are unused, how many have no overflow chain, how many have one overflow slot, etc. These values can be determined by means of the Poisson distribution, which is explained in almost any textbook on probability.

## VARIATIONS ON HASHING

In this section we will briefly introduce seven variations on the notion of hashing presented so far. The first three of these variations can be incorporated at the application programming level; the other four variations all require additional support from the operating system and thus would be transparent to applications programmers. The last three variations presented here allow the direct organization file to grow and shrink dynamically as records are added or deleted, but require special operating system features that are not commonly found.

The first variation we'll consider is **multiple-attribute hashing.** This method involves using one or more fields of the record as input to the hashing function, along with the primary key. For example, in an employee file, if the employee Social Security number tends to produce a lot of collisions under our hashing function, we could add the employee's age and year of hiring to the Social Security number and then apply the hashing function.

A second variation is the idea of **rehashing.** In this approach, we have a sequence of hashing functions to use. If the first function produces a collision when we attempt to add a new record to the file, the second function is tried. If this also produces a collision, we go to the third hashing function, and so on. When attempting to retrieve a record, we first check the location produced by the first function, then the location produced by the second function, and so on until the desired record is found or we are convinced that it is not in the file. We have already seen an example of rehashing in progressive overflow. The first function in the sequence is whatever hash function was chosen for the file, the second function is the first function plus 1, the third function is the first function plus 2, and so on. Of course, all of these additions are to be understood as being modulo the file size, to produce the wraparound effect needed.

The third variation available at the application program level is called **chained progressive overflow.** Essentially, this is chained overflow without a separate overflow area in the file. Collisions are handled by means of a linked list starting at the home address of the colliding records, but the overflow records are stored in slots that would be home addresses for other (noncolliding) records, as in progressive overflow. The gain in efficiency over progressive overflow is frequently too small to make this of much use in practice.

**Table-assisted hashing** calls for the operating system to allocate a set of buckets to hold the data records of the file along with a table for the file as part of its overhead. Each bucket would normally be expected to hold several records, and these buckets would be numbered in sequence, beginning with 0. The table would be treated basically as a one-dimensional array with one entry per bucket. (Note that the number of buckets is static and is set at the time the file is created.) The hash function, instead of producing a single address, will now produce a sequence of addresses along with a corresponding sequence of what are called signatures. A signature is nothing more than a bit string. Thus, when hashing a record key, we get a list of bucket numbers, each of which has a signature that goes with it. We can represent this result as bucket-1, bucket-2, bucket-3, . . . , bucket-n, and sign-1, sign-2, sign-3, . . . , sign-n.

To insert a new record into such a file, the algorithm checks the first bucket in the sequence produced by the hashing function for which the signature of the record is less than the table entry for the corresponding bucket. That is, we find the smallest $i$ for which sign-$i$ is less than the table entry for bucket-$i$. If there is room available in that bucket, the record is inserted and the task is finished. If not, then the records in the bucket, along with the one to be added, are put in order according to their signatures for that bucket. A separating signature value is found so that all of the records with a smaller signature will fit in the bucket. All records with signatures equal to or exceeding this separating value are overflow records, which need to be inserted in some other bucket. Any time a bucket overflows, the separating signature is put into the table entry for that bucket. Each of the overflow records is then considered for insertion into the next bucket in the sequence of bucket numbers from the hash function. That is, if a record was in its bucket-2 at the time of its overflow (based on its sign-2), the algorithm would try to add it to its bucket-3. If it overflowed there (based on its sign-3), we go to bucket-4, and so on. As you can see, it is possible for the process of adding one more record to cause a lot of moving of records in the file; insertions to table-assisted files can thus be quite costly.

Retrieving a record from a table-assisted file, however, is accomplished more efficiently. To do so, we again generate the sequences of bucket numbers and corresponding signatures from the hashing of the primary key. We then find the smallest value of $i$ such that sign-$i$ is less than the table value for bucket-$i$. We then know that bucket-$i$ is the only bucket in which the record might be, so it is the only bucket that has to be read. If the record is not in that bucket, it is not in the file. Deletions are accomplished by merely removing the record from the bucket, without changing the table or the other buckets.

Some notes are probably in order here. First, a given bucket of the file will most likely not be in the same position in all the bucket lists of different records. For example, bucket number 12 might be bucket-3 for one record, bucket-8 for another, and bucket-15 for a third. Second, trying to add one more record to a bucket can cause several records to overflow if the highest signature in the bucket is shared by those other records. Third, these overflowing records (if there are more than one) probably will not all go to the same next bucket, and even if they should happen to have the same next bucket, they will probably have different signatures for that bucket. Finally, at the time the file is created, each table entry should contain a string of all 1's, so that any record being added to the file will have a smaller signature than the table entry, at least until a bucket overflows. Of course, this means that a string of all 1's is not a legitimate signature for the hashing function to produce from any primary key.

**Virtual hashing** is the first of three examples of extensible hashing schemes that we will consider. An extensible scheme is one in which it is unnecessary to allocate all record slots at the time the file is created. Rather, it allows the file to grow and shrink dynamically as records are inserted and deleted. Of course, this requires extra support from the operating system and so it is beyond the scope of what can be decided at the application programming level. The three extensible hashing schemes presented here will be discussed only as an overview.

Interested readers should check the references at the end of this chapter for more detailed explanations.

Virtual hashing can best be explained by means of an example. Let us suppose that our hashing function is to use as the home bucket address the remainder produced by dividing record keys by a preselected number, $N$. When a particular bucket overflows, we will rehash the records in the bucket along with the record to be inserted, using remainders from division by $2N$. Thus, if $N = 50$ and bucket 27 overflows, the records involved will be rehashed using division/remainder with $2N = 100$. One immediate result of this is that we now need, say, bucket number 77 (since, for example, record key 477 hashed to 27 before, but now hashes to 77). Hence, as any bucket overflows the operating system must allocate additional buckets to the file to accommodate the expanded range of the revised hashing function. The system will also have to keep track of a history of these overflows and hashing function extensions, since some records in the file are still hashed under the original function, some under the first revision, some under the second, and so on. Through the use of this history, the proper variation of the hashing function for a given primary key can be determined.

**Dynamic hashing** involves the use of a collection of binary trees, somewhat similar to the index used in index-sequential organizations to be discussed in the next chapter. Since we have not discussed the data structure of a binary tree yet, we obviously will not treat dynamic hashing very thoroughly here. The basic idea, though, is to have the first hash function produce the address of a root node of a binary tree. A second hash function will produce a bit string, where each bit tells us whether to go to the right child or the left child as we move down the tree. Eventually, in traveling down the tree, we will arrive at a bucket containing data records for the file. This bucket is the only one that might contain the record key in question. All of the nonterminal nodes contain only pointers to nodes lower in the tree. Let us realize that this explanation could only make sense after an understanding of binary trees, which will be presented in the next chapter. Again, the operating system must be able to allocate and deallocate buckets to the file and nodes to the structure above the file as records are inserted or deleted.

**Extendible hashing** uses a hashing function that produces a bit string of a fixed length and an array called a directory. Each entry of the array contains a pointer to a bucket from the file. To access the home bucket for a record, the first part of the bit string produced by hashing its primary key is used to identify the proper directory entry. The pointer in that entry is then used to access the proper bucket. The bucket pointed to will have all of the records whose bit strings begin with the value of the directory slot number. For example, directory entry number 6 will point to the bucket containing all records whose bit strings start off with 110. If that same bucket also holds all records whose bit strings start with 111, the directory entry number 7 will also point to that bucket. If the first $n$ bits of the bit string are sufficient to identify the home bucket for that record, the directory will have $2^n$ entries. Thus, if the first four bits will distinguish the bucket for any record in the file, our directory will have sixteen entries. Again, the system must be able to dynamically allocate and deallocate buckets and directory slots as the file expands or contracts. Also, the current value for the number of bits needed to identify the proper bucket must be saved and available for the system to use.

## CONCLUDING REMARKS

Historically, the direct organization files that we have discussed here were the first computer file structures to provide users with random access. We have taken advantage of this feature to update the file in place, avoiding the need for two master files, and gain the ability to process each transaction independently of the others. Thus, the requirement to sort transactions and the logic for processing multiple transactions need no longer be issues.

The advantages of random access will also be exploited in the next chapter, where we will look at index-sequential files. We will also have the advantage of a system-maintained access structure, which was not available with direct organization files (where the program code had to determine the desired location to access). As we will see, this simplifies the algorithm considerably.

## EXERCISES

**1.** How could we modify the updating algorithms given here so as to hold each master record until all transactions for it were processed?

2. How would these algorithms need to be modified if we used absolute addressing rather than relative addressing?

3. What are the key differences between the algorithm for direct addressing and the algorithm for indirect addressing?

4. How would the indirect addressing algorithm need to be modified if we used progressive overflow instead of chained overflow?

5. Give some examples of situations for which a direct organization would be the organization of choice.

6. Suppose that our primary key values are between 300 and 499 and that there would never be more than one key in any interval of five (e.g., at most one key in 300–304, at most one in 305–309, at most one in 495–499). Design a hashing function that would have a uniform distribution.

7. Suppose we are using the prime division/remainder hashing scheme with the prime number being 5. Compute the average search length (with chained overflow and one record per slot) for the following set of primary key values: 321, 453, 263, 408, and 296. Is this average acceptable? What step(s) could be taken to improve it and still use the same basic type of hashing function?

## PROGRAMMING PROJECTS:

1. Modify the Programming Project from Chapter 3 so that it will handle the master file if it has a direct organization using relative-direct addressing.

2. Modify the programming project in Chapter 3 (or the program from the project above) to handle the master file if it has a direct organization using relative-indirect addressing. Your instructor will specify the details of the hashing function and the handling of collisions.

## OTHER READINGS

1. Bradley, James. *File and Data Base Techniques* (New York: Holt, Rinehart and Winston, 1981), pp. 61–85.

**2.**   Fagin, R., Nievergelt, J., Pippenger, N., and Strong, H. R. "Extendible Hashing—A Fast Access Method for Dynamic Files," *ACM Transactions on Database Systems,* vol. 4, no. 3 (September 1979), pp. 315–344.

**3.**   Larson, P. "Dynamic Hashing," *BIT,* vol. 18 (1978), pp. 184–201.

**4.**   Larson, P., and Kajla, A. "File Organization: Implementation of a Method Guaranteeing Retrieval in One Access," *Communications of the ACM,* vol. 27, no. 7 (July 1984), pp. 670–677.

**5.**   Litwin, W. "Virtual Hashing: A Dynamically Changing Hashing," *Proceedings of the 4th International Conference on Very Large Databases* (West Berlin, September 1978), pp. 517–523.

**6.**   Miller, Nancy. *File Structures Using Pascal* (Menlo Park, CA: Benjamin Cummings, 1987), pp. 214–216.

**7.**   Smith, Peter D., and Barnes, G. Michael. *Files and Databases: An Introduction* (Reading, MA: Addison Wesley, 1987), pp. 122–136.

# 5 MAINTAINING INDEX-SEQUENTIAL FILES

This chapter will present a user's perspective of index-sequential file maintenance using the random access available. We will briefly review the notion of index-sequential organization presented in Chapter 1. We will then consider an algorithm for updating such files, and discuss backup, recovery, and creation of index-sequential files. The chapter will present a discussion of how to simulate this organization in languages that do not support it directly, and conclude with a presentation of the data structures used to implement this organization. Before we actually begin, however, let us mention that these files are frequently referred to as ISAM files, which stands for Index Sequential Access Mode files. Although this is an abuse of terminology (since we are talking about organization rather than access mode), it is a fairly common label.

## A REVIEW OF INDEX-SEQUENTIAL ORGANIZATION

Recall from Chapter 1 that an index-sequential file is one in which records appear to be arranged in sequence by primary key value and for which the computer system maintains an index file. The index file contains records of the primary key values of actual data records and the locations of these data records in the data file. In a true index-sequential organization, the user does not see this index file. That is, the index file is transparent to the user. This organization allows for sequential access of records in order by their primary key values and for random access through the index. Perhaps the main difference between index-sequential organization and direct organization is that in index-sequential organization we use an index file look-up procedure to locate a record, while in direct organization we use some form of computation to determine the location to access.

With random access, the user supplies the key value of the desired record. The system then checks through the index file to determine the location of this record in the data file. Once the location is determined, the desired record is retrieved for the user. Searching the index file will normally be much quicker than searching the data file because the index records are so much shorter than those of the data file. Since the records are shorter, more of them will fit in main memory at one time. Thus more (if not all) of the index file can be searched before another transfer from disk is needed. Since transfers between disk and main memory are very slow (relative to other computer operations), avoiding these transfers can save a great deal of time in the execution of a program. (This will be considered in more detail in Chapter 7.)

## AN OVERVIEW OF THE ALGORITHM

Since an index-sequential file has records stored in order by primary key, we could use the algorithm from Chapter 3 to perform the update operation. In fact, if the update operation is expected to modify a very high percentage of records, this might be the more efficient approach. However, in most situations only a relatively small number of records need to be accessed in an update, so we will take advantage of the random access available here.

The approach taken here will be to process each transaction in turn. The master file will be checked for a record with the same key value as the transaction. Then the type of transaction will be used to invoke the proper module (add, change, or delete). These modules carry out the desired operation if possible or report an update error otherwise.

The algorithm presented here (as in the previous chapter) is as simple as possible. Since we are using random access, we can process each transaction independently of all the others. We don't have to worry about handling all transactions for the same master at one time (although the order in which they are processed can affect the state of the master file after the program run). Thus, as soon as a transaction is processed, the algorithm modifies the contents of the file. Again, although it is no longer crucial that the transactions be sorted before beginning the operation, it is still recommended that this sorting be done. First, as just mentioned, the effects of multiple transactions depend on their ordering. If we are going to control these effects, transactions must be sorted. Also, it turns out that the update process will be more efficient if the transactions are sorted, as will be demonstrated in Chapter 7.

As in the previous two chapters, we will assume that the transactions have been validated beforehand and that any transaction records with edit errors have been reported and removed from further consideration. We also need to realize here that there is a distinction between writing and rewriting in the algorithm. With most index-sequential organizations, if a record has been read from the file and modified, the output operation is referred to as a "rewrite." However, if the record was not previously in the file but has just been created by an add request, the operation is called a "write."

There is one last comment before we present the details of the algorithm. The syntax for file I/O operations under random access varies from one language to another, and sometimes from one computer system to another. This may necessitate some modifications to the algorithm in modules doing I/O.

---

## THE ALGORITHM IN DETAIL

### *Update an Index–Sequential File*

```
call the module to:
    initialize the counters
    open the files
call the module to:
    read a transaction {with end-of-file test}
until the transaction file is exhausted
    Apply-trans
call the module to:
    print the summary tallies
    close the files
terminate the run
```

### *Apply–trans*

```
Get-master
if   the transaction is an add request
then Attempt-add
else if    the transaction is a change request
     then   Attempt-change
     else   Attempt-delete
call the module to:
    read a transaction
```

### Get–master

```
check master file for a record with matching key
if   such a record exists
         then read record into the program variables
         turn on the master-found flag
else turn off the master-found flag
```

### Attempt–add

```
if   a matching master record was found
then report an update error
else load data into the master record variables
         write master record to the master file
```

### Attempt–change

```
if   a matching master record was found
then modify the master record
         rewrite the master record to master file
else report an update error
```

### Attempt–delete

```
if   a matching master record was found
then delete the record from the master file
else report an update error
```

## BACKING UP AND CREATING
## INDEX-SEQUENTIAL FILES

The processes for backing up and creating an index-sequential organization file are virtually identical to those for direct organization files, so we won't take the time to repeat them here. You may refer back to Chapter 4 for this information. The one main difference is that records can be added to index-sequential files without concern for available space, so in creating the template no request for a number of records would be made of the user.

# WHEN TO USE INDEX-SEQUENTIAL ORGANIZATION

We have seen that sequential organization was acceptable if most of the applications would need most of the records, since we can handle such applications with only sequential access. We have also seen that direct organization might be desirable if most of the applications would need a relatively small number of records. Random access, which we should use if we only want a few records for an application, is supported by both direct organization and index-sequential organization. As something of an oversimplification, direct organization files provide faster access but require more complicated programs than index-sequential organization files. The direct organization programs are more complicated because the programmer is responsible for specifying the location of the record. In contrast, the system is responsible for this with index-sequential files. The access is (generally) quicker with direct organization because the location is determined by manipulations and calculations done inside the program rather than by searching the index file. Hence the decision whether to employ index-sequential organization or direct organization often is based on the relative importance of execution speed and program development time. Recall, however, that the time advantage is not as great as it used to be and that this time advantage is lost if overflow searching must be done. Recall also that not all programming languages support index-sequential files. One further aspect that should be kept in mind is that index-sequential organization usually is set up to return records in primary key order under sequential access. Direct organization files with indirect addressing normally will not have records in primary key order. Thus, a report generation program on a hashed file might need to generate a temporary file, sort this file, and then write to the actual output file or device in order to present its data in the desired sequence.

# SIMULATING INDEX-SEQUENTIAL ORGANIZATION

If you are working in a language that does not support index-sequential organization but wish to use it anyway, you will need to include some extra operations in your program code. Basically, the simulation is done by using a direct organization for the data file. The programmer then assumes the responsibility for accessing, using, and maintaining the index file. The index file could be set up as an array-type structure containing the record key and the relative address for each record. If this index file is not overly large, the program could open it, read it into a program array structure, and then use it during execution. Before terminating its execution, the program must write the array structure back to the index file and close it. A more sophisticated data structure could be used to hold the index file to improve search time. (This is what would be done at the operating system level to maintain an actual index-sequential file.)

## IMPLEMENTING INDEX-SEQUENTIAL ORGANIZATION

This section will discuss the data structures used to implement index-sequential organization. We will begin with a review of binary search trees, including their structure and processing for storing ordered data. We will then generalize this concept to the B-tree structure, with a very brief mention of the B*-tree structure. The modification of the B-tree structure to the B$^+$-tree structure will be shown, along with some possible variations of B$^+$-trees. The section will conclude with a brief description of IBM's VSAM (Virtual Storage Access Mode) structure.

### Binary Search Trees

A binary tree consists of a collection of nodes, each of which has a data area to hold the information being stored and two pointer areas. The pointer areas hold the addresses of the left and right children of the node. The tree has one node at the top that is called the root of the tree. Each node within the tree is the root of the subtree that consists of itself and all of its descendants. A node that has no children is called a leaf. (Note that we have an upside-down tree here, with the root at the top of the diagram and the leaves at the bottom.) If a node does not have a left or right child, the pointer area for that child will contain a null value.

If the binary tree is being used to maintain data in some particular order, the standard arrangement of data is as follows: all data in a node's left subtree (that is, in the subtree whose root is the left child) come before the node's data in the ordering, while all data in the right subtree come after the node's data. Figure 5.1 shows a binary search tree where the data are people's first names and the ordering is alphabetical.

**FIGURE 5.1**  *Binary Search Tree*

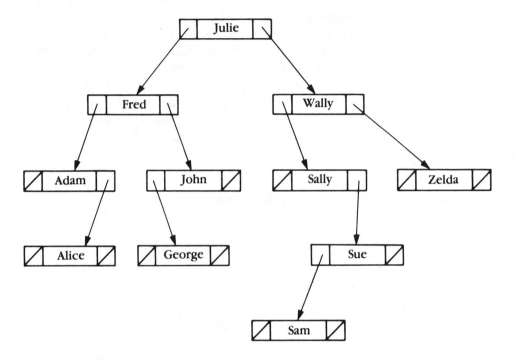

Inserting new data into a binary search tree is understood most easily by means of recursion. If the tree is empty, of course, we create a root node with two null pointers and store the data. If the tree is not empty, we set current to the tree's root, create a node pointed to by new, load our data into new (data), and set new (left) and new (right) to null. We then use the following recursive scheme. This assumes that the problem of duplicate data is not a concern here.

### Insert (current)

```
if   new (data) < current (data)
then if   current (left) is null
     then current (left)  <<-- new
     else insert (current (left))
else if   current (right) is null
     then current (right)  <<-- new
     else insert (current (right))
```

Notice that each new data item inserted into the tree will be stored in a leaf node. Figure 5.2 shows the result of this algorithm for inserting the name "Seth" into the tree.

Deleting data from a tree is also fairly easy if its node has at least one null pointer. The first task, of course, is to locate the node having the data to delete (let's call its location d-n, for delete node). If the node is a leaf, we set its parent's pointer to null and dispose of the node. If the node has exactly one non-null pointer, we copy that pointer into the parent's pointer and dispose of the node. Figure 5.3 shows the result of deleting Sally from the tree in Figure 5.2. If the node has two children, we find the largest value in the left subtree (let's call its location l-v, for largest value). The l-v node will be found by following

**FIGURE 5.2** *Binary Search Tree After Insertion*

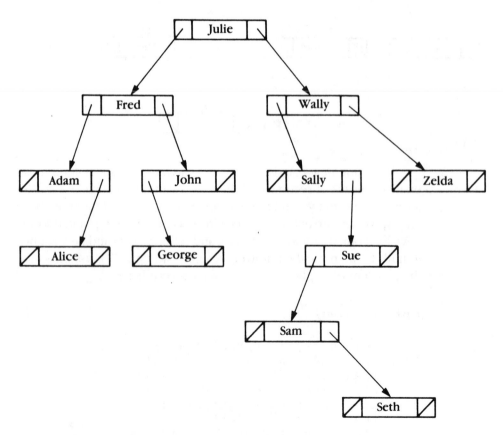

**FIGURE 5.3   *Binary Search Tree After Deletion***

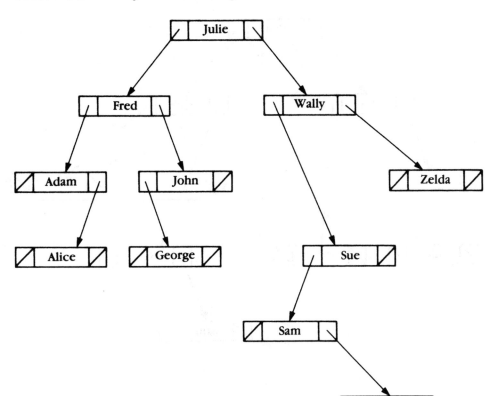

the left pointer from d-n, then following right pointers until we get to
a node without a right pointer. This node is l-v. The data of l-v are
copied into d-n, and then l-v is deleted from the tree. Figure 5.4 shows
the result of deleting Julie from the tree in Figure 5.3.

With this understanding of the structure of a binary search tree
and its insertion and deletion algorithms, we should now discuss the
"in-order" transversal algorithm. In traversing the tree, we want to
perform some type of processing on each data item stored in the tree
and we want the processing done according to the proper ordering
of this data. This is done by setting current equal to the root of the
tree (assuming that the tree is not empty) and calling the recursive
routine shown here.

**FIGURE 5.4**  *Binary Search Tree After Deletion*

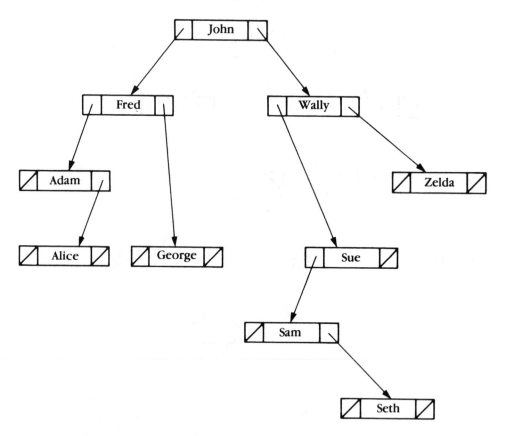

***Traverse (current)***

```
if   current (left) is non-null
then traverse (current (left))

process current (data)

if   current (right) is non-null
then traverse (current (right))
```

Using this algorithm on any of the four figures shown above should produce a list of all names in the tree in alphabetical order. Binary search trees are often used for storing ordered data because they tend to be much quicker than linked lists for accessing a required node. Notice that although the tree in Figure 5.1 has eleven nodes, we never need to examine more than five nodes in looking for a given name, and in many cases we must examine only three or four.

This efficiency in searching can be improved by requiring that the tree be perfectly balanced, meaning that, from any node in the tree, the number of nodes in the right subtree can differ from the number of nodes in the left subtree by one at most. This maximizes our search efficiency in a binary tree, since distances along any two paths are as equal as possible. If we have $n$ nodes in a tree, the longest path will have a length that is the $\log_2(m)$, where $m$ is the smallest number that is a power of 2 and is strictly larger than $n$. For example, if $n$ is 14 then $m$ is 16, and the maximum path is of length 4. However, if $n$ is 32 then $m$ is 64, and the maximum path is of length 6. All paths from the root to a leaf will have a length equal to or one less than this maximum.

Naturally, there is a tradeoff for this gain in search efficiency, and that is the complexity of the insertion and deletion algorithms needed to maintain the balance. And, of course, if the algorithms are more complicated, they are harder to code and debug and will use more run time during execution. We can get something of a compromise if we use an AVL tree (named for the two people who devised it, Adel'son-Vel'skii and Landis) instead of a perfectly balanced tree. In an AVL tree, the requirement is that, for each node in the tree, the height of the right subtree differs from the height of the left subtree by one at most. The height of a tree is the maximum of the distances from the root to each leaf. The maximum distance from root to leaf in an AVL tree is the same as for a perfectly balanced tree, but an AVL tree can have more paths at this maximum length than a perfectly balanced tree, particularly if the number of nodes is just barely larger than a power of 2. Figure 5.5 shows an AVL tree with 17 nodes. Note that the maximum length of five accesses is attained along five paths, while two paths require four, and one path requires three accesses. Figure 5.6 shows a perfectly balanced tree of seventeen nodes, with only two paths of maximum length and all other paths having a length that is one less than the maximum. As a general rule, an AVL tree will be slightly less efficient for searching than a perfectly balanced tree but will be noticeably more efficient for insertion and deletion operations because of its simpler algorithm.

## B-Trees

In the binary search tree, we have one data item and two pointers in each node; all data in the left subtree of a node have smaller values

**FIGURE 5.5** *AVL Tree*

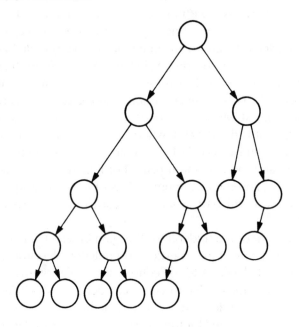

**FIGURE 5.6** *Perfectly Balanced Tree*

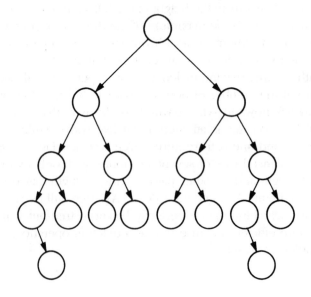

and all data in the right subtree have larger values. The idea of a B-tree is to extend this structure to larger nodes while maintaining the sorted arrangement of the binary search tree and the balancing of the AVL tree. Thus, a B-tree is a tree in which:

*1.* each node has space for $m - 1$ data items and $m$ pointers;

*2.* each non-leaf node has one more non-null pointer than it has data items;

*3.* unless the tree is empty, the root node has at least one data item (and at least two non-null pointers, unless it is also a leaf);

*4.* all leaves are at the same level;

*5.* in any given node, the data items are in increasing order from left to right;

*6.* the pointer to the left of a data item leads to a subtree whose data items are all smaller, and the pointer to the right leads to a subtree whose data items are all larger; and

*7.* all non-root nodes have at least truncate $((m - 1)/2)$ data items, where truncate $(x)$ is the integer part of $x$. To illustrate this, if $m = 35$, then $(m - 1)/2 = 17$, and truncate $(17) = 17$ data items per node. If $m = 46$, then $(m - 1)/2 = 22.5$, and truncate $(22.5) = 22$.

To insert a new data item into the B-tree, we locate the leaf node in which it belongs by starting at the root node and following pointers chosen by comparing our new data item with the items in each node we encounter. If there is still room in the leaf node at which we arrive, we insert our data, possibly with a movement of items within the node to maintain the proper ordering. If the leaf node into which we want to insert the data is full, we need to split that node into two nodes. Considering the $m$ data items we now have in their proper order, we pick the "middle" (or median) item. The data items less than the "middle" remain in the leaf node at which we arrived. The data items larger than the "middle" item are put into a newly created node, which becomes another leaf in the tree. The "middle" item itself is no longer stored in a leaf node, but is inserted into the parent of the leaf node that we split. This insertion may again require moving data within the parent node to maintain the proper ordering. If the parent node is already full, this node will need to be split also, moving its "middle" item up another level in the B-tree. Notice, then, that, as in the binary tree, data are always inserted into a leaf node. However, unlike the binary tree, the new leaf is not at a lower level than the previous node, but at the same level. The height of the B-tree increases by splitting nodes and moving data upward, eventually leading to a new root node as a parent of the node that had previously been the root.

Deleting data from a B-tree is also analogous to deleting data from a binary tree, with some modifications for the multiple data items per node. To handle a deletion request, we must first locate the data to remove by starting at the root and following the appropriate pointers down the B-tree. If the deletion data is not in a leaf, we replace it with the smallest data item in the larger subtree to which it points. We then move down to this subtree and delete the data that has been moved up. This process is repeated until we eventually have to delete data from a leaf. If this deletion does not bring us below the minimum number of data items, then there is no further work involved. If we do fall below the minimum number of data items, we combine this leaf with an adjacent leaf having the same parent. If the adjacent leaf was at the minimum size, the two leaves will become one. If combining the leaves involves too many data items to fit into one node, the two leaves each get as close as possible to half the data items. In either case, the pointers and data values in the parent node will be adjusted.

Figure 5.7 shows a B-tree of depth 2 and $m = 6$. The data illustrated in the nodes are only the key values; in an actual B-tree, full data records are stored there. Notice that each node has space for five data values and six pointers, and actually contains between two and five data items, which is required for all nodes except the root. Notice also that left subtrees have only smaller values and right subtrees have only larger values, and that each data item not in a leaf has both a right and a left subtree associated with it. Figure 5.8 shows the result of having first inserted 540 (which did not require any restructuring of the B-tree) and then inserting 760, with the resulting tree growth. Before reading further, follow the insertion algorithm above to verify that Figure 5.8 is correct. (In splitting a set of six data items into two nodes, the fourth item is being used as the one in the "middle" in these examples.)

Figure 5.9 shows the effect of deleting records 450 and 900, which does not require any structural changes to the B-tree of Figure 5.8. Notice, however, that record 910 has been moved from one node to another as a result of this deletion.

Figure 5.10 shows the result of deleting record 410, with the rearranging of data items in the leaf nodes and the parent node but no structural changes. The effects of deleting record 930 are also shown, with the merging of two leaves into one and the adjustments to the parent and grandparent nodes. While not illustrated here, realize that

**FIGURE 5.7** *B-Tree*

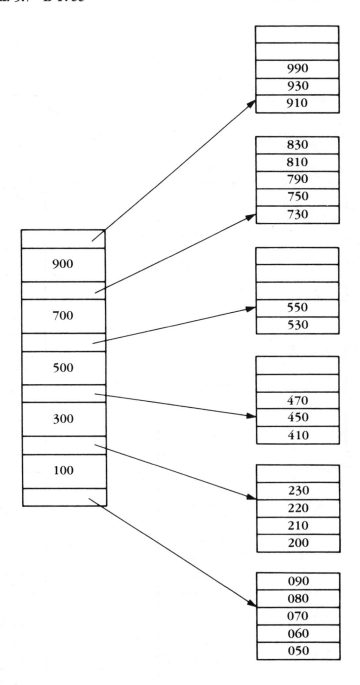

**FIGURE 5.8**  *B-Tree After Insertion*

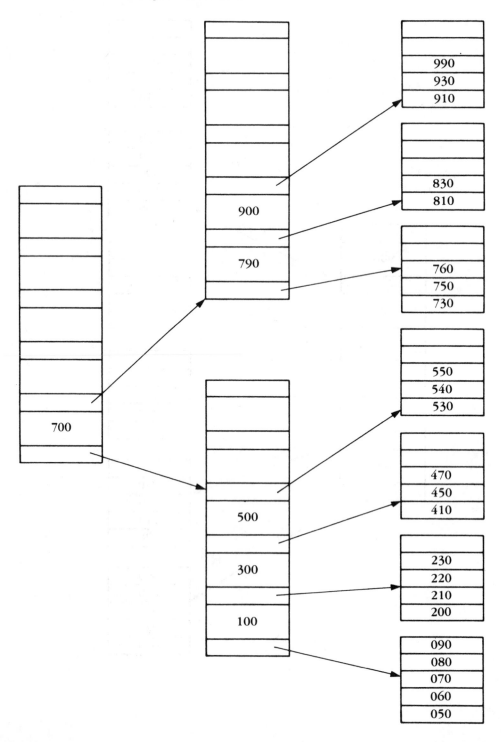

**FIGURE 5.9   *B-Tree After Deletion***

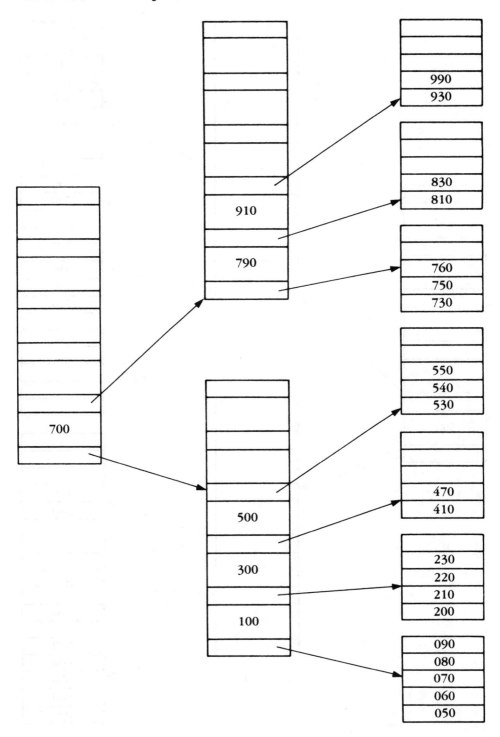

**FIGURE 5.10**   *B-Tree After Deletion*

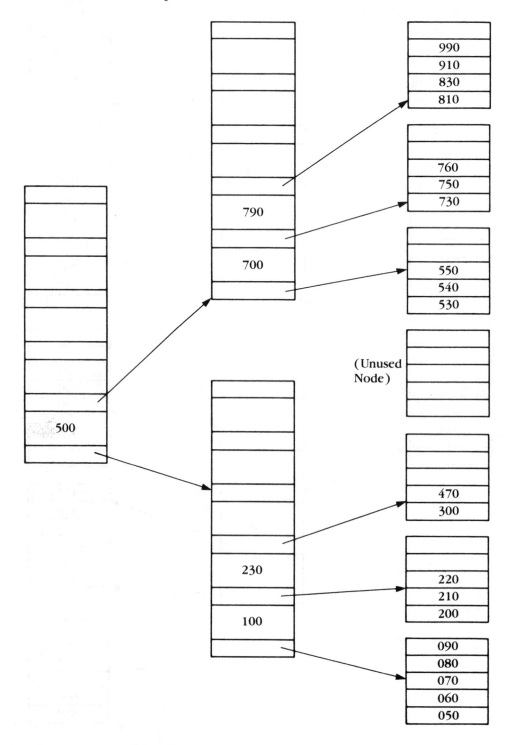

the merging caused by deletion may cascade all the way to the root, thus reducing the height of the B-tree. Again, you should trace through the effects of these deletions to verify that Figure 5.10 will be the state of the B-tree after the removals are completed.

Note that a node created as a leaf will always remain a leaf node. There is never an occasion for a leaf node to become a parent in the processing of a B-tree. (The one exception to this is the first node created when the B-tree is originally established. At that time, the single node is both a leaf and the root. If we focus on its role as the root rather than as a leaf, the statement above remains true.) With this observation, we realize that leaf nodes do not need to contain pointer fields at all, since they will never use pointer values. Thus we can consider two distinct data types for nodes. In fact, Figures 5.7 through 5.10 reflect this distinction.

As a final comment on B-trees, note that the processing of data in proper order is done by a generalization of the in-order traversal used in binary search trees. Viewing each non-leaf node as an alternating sequence of pointers and data items, we (recursively) traverse the left subtree, process the data item, and traverse the right subtree. In this manner we can access each data item in its proper place in the sorting sequence.

## B*-Trees

While the algorithms to process a B*-tree are more complicated than what we wish to discuss here, the basic idea of this structure is easy to comprehend once one has come to terms with the idea of a B-tree. In a B-tree, the splitting of nodes was done as soon as the maximum capacity of a node was about to be exceeded. In this way, nodes are always between half full and completely full, with an expectation of 75 percent utilization of space in the B-tree. In a B*-tree, we postpone splitting nodes until the node and those adjacent to it (belonging to the same parent) are full. This requires more movement of data, but it delays splitting and ensures that each node will be at least two-thirds full, improving the utilization of space in the structure. Naturally, this saving in space comes at the cost of more complex algorithms and increased processing time for insertions and deletions.

## B+-Trees and Index-Sequential Files

A much more important variation (for our purposes, at least) of the B-tree is the notion of a B+-tree. This structure is the same as a B-tree except that actual data records are stored only in the leaves. The parent nodes of the B+-tree contain only primary key values and pointers. More precisely, a B+-tree is a data structure that:

**1.**  stores all data in leaf nodes, with each leaf having sufficient space to hold $r$ records;

**2.**  will have at least truncate ($r/2$) records in each leaf, with the records in sequence by primary key value;

**3.**  has space for $m$ pointers and $m - 1$ primary key values in each non-leaf node, with the key values in sequential order;

**4.**  will have one more non-null pointer than the number of key values in each non-leaf node;

**5.**  will have at least truncate (($m - 1$)/2) key values in each non-leaf node (except for the root, which might have only one key value); and

**6.**  will have all key values in the left subtree less than the given key, and all key values in the right subtree larger.

Frequently, in addition to the pointers of the non-leaf nodes of the B+-tree, we will have pointers in the leaf nodes to form a linked list of these nodes. Thus, we can access all records in sequential order by primary key value without having to traverse the entire B+-tree.

The B+-tree is obviously a useful structure for implementing the index-sequential organization. Of course, the actual data file is stored in physical blocks on disk. These blocks are taken as the leaf nodes of a B+-tree. The non-leaf nodes constitute the index file (which is maintained by the operating system through the file management software). Random access is achieved by supplying a primary key value to the system, which will begin a descent into the B+-tree, comparing the given key to the key values in the nodes encountered until it arrives at the pointer to the disk block that contains the desired record (if this record is actually in the file). This block can then be transferred to main memory and searched for the record in question.

Sequential access is achieved by avoiding the B+-tree structure and accessing the record blocks through the linked list of leaf nodes.

The algorithms for inserting and deleting records is essentially the same as those for the B-tree.

## Some Variations on the B+-Tree Structure

As with any linked data structure, B+-trees have what might seem like 1,001 variations, although the actual number is probably smaller than that. We'll consider five possible variations here, some of which are used by computer vendors in their operating systems for implementing index-sequential files. It is in this context that the term ISAM (Index Sequential Access Mode) originated.

One possible variation would be to avoid the left-most pointer in the non-leaf nodes. In this situation, the number of pointers is equal to the number of primary key values (both in actuality and in potential) in each non-leaf node. The key values are still in order within each node and each pointer leads to a sub-tree whose key values are no larger than the key value immediately preceding the pointer. Thus, the key values in the non-leaf nodes would be the largest key of the sub-tree, each followed by a pointer to that sub-tree.

Another variation would avoid the splitting of leaf-nodes as new data records were added to the file. This can be accomplished by linking leaf-nodes together to form overflow chains. When the original leaf becomes full, the next insertion that belongs in that node is put into an overflow node and the original leaf gets a pointer to the overflow node. This simplifies the insertion process but can slow down the retrieval process.

It is possible, if the linking of overflow leaves is done, to limit the number of levels in the $B^+$-tree, either to a maximum value or to a fixed value. For example, if it is predetermined that there will be at most sixty-four leaf-nodes (each with the potential for overflow nodes linked to it), and if each non-leaf node is set up to accommodate four pointers, then the non-leaf portion of the $B^+$-tree would never need more than three levels. If we abandon the minimum space utilization requirements, we can mandate exactly three levels at all times.

In a different vein, it is possible to mark records as "deleted" without actually removing the data from the $B^+$-tree structure. This of course saves time in the updating process but it does not free up space for new data. It also means that there will be more items to check during retrieval operations, as well as additional program code to check for the deleted markers and to ignore the associated records. These "deleted" records would actually be removed only when the file is reorganized.

The final variation we will mention here involves separating the key value from the rest of the data of the record (in the leaf nodes). In this approach, the key values would be at one end of the node and each value would have a pointer to that part of the node that contains the data of the associated record. This permits the searching of a smaller area of the node to find the specific record desired.

## VSAM

So far in this text, we have avoided a discussion of particular systems or products on the market and have focused instead on the underlying concepts used by these systems and products. The one exception to this policy will be our brief overview of IBM's VSAM presented here, which is included only because the term is fairly widely known and used in the field of file processing. VSAM is an acronym for Virtual Storage Access Mode (a misnomer, as was ISAM) and is produced and marketed by IBM. VSAM is essentially an umbrella-type structure that offers three options within this type of file. The first option available is the *entry-sequenced file,* which is, to all intents and purposes, a sequential organization as discussed in Chapter 3. The second option is called the *relative record file* and amounts to a direct organization with relative addressing. The third option is the *key-sequenced file,* which is a form of index-sequential organization.

## CONCLUDING REMARKS

We have now concluded our discussion of file updating procedures. A useful activity would be to compare and contrast the algorithms used with each of the three file organizations and note their similarities and differences.

    This also bring us to the point where we will shift emphasis away from the application programmer's point of view and consider structures and devices that underlie the file organizations presented but which are not normally of concern at the application level. Indeed, one can write programs for file maintenance and file retrieval quite adequately in most situations without any real knowledge of the data structures or hardware used to implement the files. The tree structures discussed in this chapter, along with those discussed in Chapter 6 and the hardware covered in Chapter 7, would be of concern to application programmers only in the context of efficiency concerns.

## EXERCISES

1. Explain the index-sequential organization in your own words.
2. Explain why the index file is "transparent to the user."

3. Explain the process the system uses to retrieve a record from an index-sequential file.

4. Why is it generally quicker to search the index file for a key value than it is to search the data file for that key?

5. Why is it not absolutely necessary to sort the transactions before running the update operation?

6. What are the two reasons why it is a good idea to sort the transactions anyway?

7. Why can we perform the output to the file immediately after processing a transaction in index-sequential organization, when in sequential organization we have to wait until all transactions for a master record are done to perform the output?

8. In your own words, explain the algorithm given in this chapter for updating an index-sequential file.

9. How could this algorithm be modified to hold each master record until all transactions for it had been applied?

10. What would we expect to gain from this modification? What would we expect to lose?

11. Explain the process of backing up an index-sequential file.

12. Explain the process of creating an index-sequential file.

13. Under what circumstances should index-sequential organization be picked for a file? Give an example where index-sequential organization would work well and two examples where it wouldn't (one calling for sequential organization and one calling for direct organization).

14. Explain how to simulate a file with index-sequential organization in a language that does not support it. Why might we want to do this?

15. Explain why "ISAM" is technically an incorrect label.

16. Explain how data are arranged in a binary search tree. Where is new data inserted into an existing tree? In what manner is data retrieved from a binary search tree so that it can be processed in its proper order?

17. Why is balancing important in a binary search tree?

18. What is the distinction between a perfectly balanced tree and an AVL tree? What are the advantages and disadvantages of each?

19. Define a B-tree in your own words. How is the growth of a B-tree different from the growth of a binary search tree?

20.  Insert 075, 240, and 207 into the B-tree in Figure 5.8.

21.  Delete 930 from the B-tree in Figure 5.9.

22.  Traverse the B-tree in Figure 5.8 (as it was before Exercise 20), listing the items in the order they are to be processed by this traversal.

23.  Explain in your own words the distinction between a B-tree and a B*-tree.

24.  Define a B+-tree in your own words. Convert the B-tree in Figure 5.7 to a B+-tree. Append a name to each identification number to show the difference between the data nodes and the pointer nodes in your B+-tree. Trace the insertions and deletions to the B-tree shown in Figures 5.8 through 5.10 on your B+-tree.

## PROGRAMMING PROJECT

Modify the program from Chapter 3 (or one of the programs from Chapter 4) to update an index-sequential file.

## OTHER READINGS

1.  Aho, A., Hopcroft, J., and Ullman, J. *Data Structures and Algorithms* (Reading, MA: Addison-Wesley Publishing Co., 1987).

2.  Claybrook, B. *File Management Techniques* (New York: John Wiley & Sons, 1983), Chapters 4 and 5.

3.  Peterson, W., and Lew, A. *File Design and Programming* (New York: John Wiley & Sons, 1986), Chapter 5.

# 6 SECONDARY KEY ACCESS

As we mentioned in Chapter 1, each record in a data file normally has a primary key field, which acts as a unique identifier for that record. We also noted that the "labels" we use in everyday life as identifiers (such as people's names) are not necessarily unique, so we invent identification numbers to be used as primary keys. Because these identification numbers are rather artificial and arbitrarily selected, it sometimes happens that the primary key value of a needed record is not known, which leads to the need for access via a secondary key. A secondary key is used to identify records in a manner that is not necessarily unique, so secondary key access must be able to cycle efficiently through all of the records having the requested value in the secondary key field. With some secondary keys, such as full name, we would expect very little duplication, so the identifier is almost unique. Other types of secondary keys, such as the street on which a person lives or the department of the company in which he or she works, will have a much higher rate of duplication.

In this chapter we will consider some of the data structures that could be used in the file manager portion of the operating system to provide secondary key access to files. Since we will want to have random access to the file, secondary key access is only appropriate for index-sequential or direct organization files. Of course, the designation of a field as a secondary key would need to be done at the time the template for the file is created, since these data structures are part of the file structure overhead.

The data structures that we will present here are inverted files (both fully inverted and partially inverted) and multilists.

## INVERTED FILES

An inverted file provides random access for records based on secondary key values by means of a second file (or table) containing the values of the secondary key field and pointers to the records in the data file that have that value. When the user supplies the desired value, the system can check that value in the inverted file structure to locate records that have that value. These records can be displayed to the user, one at a time, until the desired record is located (or until all records are processed, whichever is appropriate). If the inverted file contains pointers to all data records with a given value, it is said to be *fully inverted.* If the inverted file has a pointer to the "first" appropriate data record, with the data records chained together as a linked list, then it is said to be *partially inverted.* Figure 6.1 shows a student data file (without any secondary key access structure). Figures 6.2(a)–(c)

**FIGURE 6.1   A Student Data File**

| Record Number | Student ID Number | Major | Status |
|---|---|---|---|
| 0 | 203 | Math | Junior |
| 1 | 307 | CS | Freshman |
| 2 | 504 | CS | Sophomore |
| 3 | 609 | English | Freshman |
| 4 | 717 | Math | Senior |
| 5 | 849 | CS | Junior |
| 6 | 985 | CS | Freshman |

**FIGURE 6.2(a)   Fully Inverted Data File**

| Record Number | Student ID Number | Major | Status |
|---|---|---|---|
| 0 | 203 | 0 | 2 |
| 1 | 307 | 1 | 0 |
| 2 | 504 | 1 | 1 |
| 3 | 609 | 2 | 0 |
| 4 | 717 | 0 | 3 |
| 5 | 849 | 1 | 2 |
| 6 | 985 | 1 | 0 |

**FIGURE 6.2(b)**   *Fully Inverted File on Major*

| Record Number | Major | Location of Data Records |
|---|---|---|
| 0 | Math | 0, 4 |
| 1 | CS | 1, 2, 5, 6 |
| 2 | English | 3 |

**FIGURE 6.2(c)**   *Fully Inverted File on Status*

| Record Number | Status | Location of Data Records |
|---|---|---|
| 0 | Freshman | 1, 3, 6 |
| 1 | Sophomore | 2 |
| 2 | Junior | 0, 5 |
| 3 | Senior | 4 |

show a student data file fully inverted on major and status, while Figures 6.3(a)–(c) show the same file partially inverted on these two fields. Notice in Figures 6.2 and 6.3 that the actual value of the secondary key is contained only in the inverted file and not in the data file. In place of the value in the data file, we have a pointer to the record of the

**FIGURE 6.3(a)**   *Partially Inverted Data File*

| Record Number | Student ID Number | Major | Next Major | Status | Next Status |
|---|---|---|---|---|---|
| 0 | 203 | 0 | 4 | 2 | 5 |
| 1 | 307 | 1 | 2 | 0 | 3 |
| 2 | 504 | 1 | 5 | 1 | 2 |
| 3 | 609 | 2 | 3 | 0 | 6 |
| 4 | 717 | 0 | 0 | 3 | 4 |
| 5 | 849 | 1 | 6 | 2 | 0 |
| 6 | 985 | 1 | 1 | 0 | 1 |

**FIGURE 6.3(b)   *Partially Inverted File on Major***

| Record Number | Major | First Data Record |
|---|---|---|
| 0 | Math | 0 |
| 1 | CS | 1 |
| 2 | English | 3 |

**FIGURE 6.3(c)   *Partially Inverted File on Status***

| Record Number | Status | First Data Record |
|---|---|---|
| 0 | Freshman | 1 |
| 1 | Sophomore | 2 |
| 2 | Junior | 0 |
| 3 | Senior | 4 |

inverted file that has the desired secondary key value. The record number columns shown here are not data within the file, but are listed for ease of reference in reading these figures.

## MULTILISTS

Another method for allowing access by secondary keys is through the multilist structure. In this approach, all of the records having the same value of the secondary key are connected together in the data file as a linked list. The term multilist is used to indicate that we are allowed several different secondary key fields, each of which will have an associated pointer field. The pointer field for any given secondary key will be used for the numerous linked lists, one list per value of that secondary key. As with any linked-list structure, there will have to be external pointers to the first entry in each list. Figures 6.4(a) and (b) show a multilist structure for students using the same data used in Figure 6.1. Notice that the values of the secondary keys are included

**FIGURE 6.4(a)**  *Multilist Data File*

| Record Number | Student ID Number | Major | Next Major | Status | Next Status |
|---|---|---|---|---|---|
| 0 | 203 | Math | 4 | Junior | 5 |
| 1 | 307 | CS | 2 | Freshman | 3 |
| 2 | 504 | CS | 5 | Sophomore | 2 |
| 3 | 609 | English | 3 | Freshman | 6 |
| 4 | 717 | Math | 0 | Senior | 4 |
| 5 | 849 | CS | 6 | Junior | 0 |
| 6 | 985 | CS | 1 | Freshman | 1 |

**FIGURE 6.4(b)**  *External Pointers for the Multilist*

| First Record For: | | |
|---|---|---|
| | Math | 0 |
| | CS | 1 |
| | English | 3 |
| | | |
| | Freshman | 1 |
| | Sophomore | 2 |
| | Junior | 0 |
| | Senior | 4 |

along with their pointers in the data file. Also note that we are not necessarily assuming that the external pointers are implemented in another file. Thus, a multilist is the same as a partially inverted file structure, except that the data values are included in the data records (instead of pointers back to the inverted file) and that the "inverted file" need not be a separate structure. If the linked lists in the multilist structure are circular (meaning that the last item in each linked list points back to the first item, instead of having a null pointer), then we call the structure a ring. In the ring structure, once we have accessed any record by any means, we can access all other records having the same value of a given secondary key. In the multilist or inverted file structures, it is more complicated to get all records on a given secondary key value unless that key value was used to access the original record.

## CONCLUDING REMARKS

This chapter, though quite a bit shorter than the other chapters in the book, covers all the basics of how secondary key access can be provided. This is done by some type of linked data structure, in which all records with a given secondary key value are connected to each other. As mentioned earlier, there are always multitudinous variations on any linked data structure. The four mentioned here for secondary key access are (1) partially inverted files, (2) fully inverted files, (3) multilists, and (4) rings. As you can see from the discussion, these four structures are really quite similar. Of course, system manufacturers are apt to include their own variations of these data structures for their machines and operating systems, but the differences will typically be rather minor.

## EXERCISES

1. Define a fully inverted file. Give an example of a file with at least two secondary keys that is set up as a fully inverted file.

2. Define a partially inverted file. Convert your example from Exercise 1 into a partially inverted file.

3. Define a multilist. Convert your example from Exercise 1 into a multilist structure.

4. Define a ring. Convert the multilist of Exercise 3 into a ring structure.

## OTHER READINGS

1. Aho, A., Hopcroft, J., and Ullman, J. *Data Structures and Algorithms;* (Reading, MA: Addison-Wesley Publishing Co., 1987).

2. Claybrook, B. *File Management Techniques* (New York: John Wiley & Sons, 1983), Chapters 4 and 5.

3. Peterson, W., and Lew, A. *File Design and Programming* (New York: John Wiley & Sons, 1986), Chapter 5.

# 7 HARDWARE CONSIDERATIONS

In this chapter we will be considering the computer hardware that relates to file processing, some of its characteristics, and what this means for file implementation and processing efficiency. The first three sections deal with secondary storage devices. We then look at main memory (sometimes called primary storage or core memory) and give an overview of how data are transferred between secondary storage and main memory. We conclude by discussing the implications of this on efficiency of file processing and then introducing the idea of variable-length records and their implementation.

## MAGNETIC TAPE

The magnetic tapes used on computer systems are very similar to those used in tape recorders in both appearance and general characteristics. As with tape recorders, computers now have both reel-to-reel tape drives and cassette tape drives. Data are stored on the tape by a read-write head as the tape passes through it. The data can later be retrieved from the tape by the read-write head as the tape passes through it again. However, the tape is a sequential medium for data storage. In order to access a particular item of data, one must put the tape on the tape drive and (for reel-to-reel drives at least) start at the beginning of the tape. All of the tape before the desired item must pass through the read-write head (and be read and checked by the computer, unless a tape address is known somehow) until the desired item is located.

Because of their sequential nature and because a human computer operator must install a tape before it is used, tapes are typically used for backup and archive files rather than for operational files. Furthermore, if tape is used for an operational file, that file must have a sequential organization, which prevents random access. Despite these limitations, magnetic tapes are quite good for backup and archive files, as well as for distribution of data and programs to other computer installations. These tapes are inexpensive and quite transportable.

A schematic drawing of a reel-to-reel tape drive is shown in Figure 7.1. The one variation from a tape recorder setup is the use of two vacuum chambers, one on either side of the read-write head. Because of the very high speeds at which the tape moves through the head and

**FIGURE 7.1**   *Tape Drive Schematic*

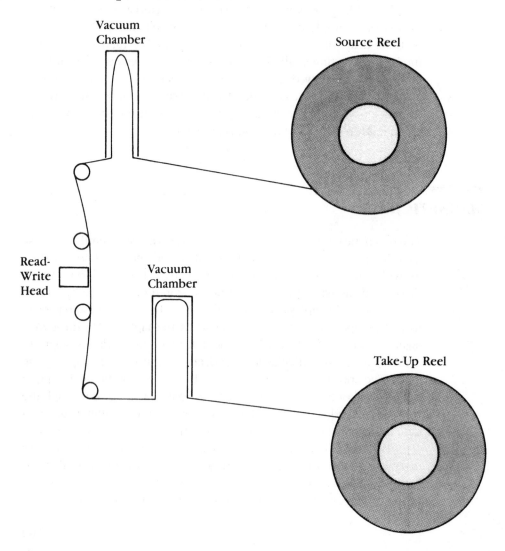

the sudden starts and stops to which it is subjected, the tape must be able to take up and create slack between the head and the reels and still maintain tension in these places. The vacuum chambers provide this "slack under tension" needed to keep the tape moving without having it snap under the sudden pulls it experiences.

The figure shows a single read-write head that is capable of either operation, but only one at a time. In some of the more sophisticated tape drives we find two heads, the first for writing only and the second for reading only. This allows the system to verify the data being written to the tape. As the first head is writing data to the tape from the computer, the second head is reading it and transmitting it back to the computer for comparison with what was sent. Thus, any data transmission error (caused by static electricity or a blemish on the tape) can be detected and corrected immediately.

The tape itself is shown in Figure 7.2. Notice that the length of the tape is divided into nine strips, called tracks. Each track will hold one bit of each character stored on the tape, while each character will take up one small portion of the tape, crossing all tracks. Nine tracks are used because the EBCDIC (Extended Binary Coded Decimal Interchange Code) uses eight bits to represent each character and a ninth bit to check for parity in some cases. The other main coding scheme, ASCII (American Standard Code for Information Interchange), uses seven bits to represent each character and an eighth bit for parity. The parity bit is used to check the validity of the character to which it is attached. When a character is stored (or sent over a data communication

**FIGURE 7.2** *A Small Section of Magnetic Tape*

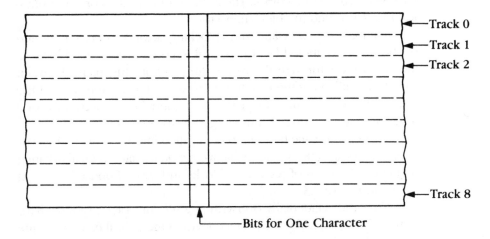

Track 0
Track 1
Track 2

Track 8

Bits for One Character

line), the number of 1s in the representation of the character are counted and the parity bit is set accordingly. Under odd parity, the total number of 1s should be odd. Thus the parity bit is set to 0 if the count from the character is already odd, and the parity bit is set to 1 if the count is even. Even parity works in a similar manner, but requires that the total number of 1s be even. With parity checking, if one of the bits in the character gets changed by a transmission error, the system can detect that error and request a retransmission of the character. The error would be detected if the character received did not have the proper parity.

A typical density for data on a tape is 1,600 cpi (that is, 1,600 characters per inch), although some (usually older) tape drives operate at 800 cpi. Of course, as the technology improves, higher densities (such as 6,400 cpi) are becoming commonplace. In some sources you may see densities measured in bpi (bits per inch). While this may cause confusion, the density measures are really the same since all the bits of one character lie on one strip across the tape. Thus, counting characters or counting bits (along one track) provides the same value. Particularly for file processing, we think of these characters as forming records. We now need to refer to these as logical records, since they represent data in our logical view of the file. The tape drive, however, works not in terms of logical records but in terms of a fixed number of characters. The number of characters associated with the tape drive is usually the number of characters that can be transmitted without interruption during an input/output operation. These units of fixed size are called physical records or blocks. When data are sent to or received from the tape drive, an entire block is transmitted. In most applications, logical records are shorter than blocks, so several logical records are packaged together in a block. The number of logical records per physical block is called the blocking factor.

Figure 7.3 shows a tape with a blocking factor of three, as indicated by the sections labeled LR (for Logical Record) inside each block. As the tape moves through the read-write head, it must pause between each block, allowing the data to be transferred to another part of the system before continuing. Since the tape cannot be stopped and started instantaneously, but needs time to get up to speed or come to a halt, we have unused space between blocks called interblock gaps (IBG) or interrecord gaps (IRG). Thus, what we get on the tape is an alternating sequence of groups of records in blocks and gaps of unused space, as shown in Figure 7.3.

To avoid accidentally overwriting a file, most tape systems have some sort of physical write-protect device. One typical example is the

**FIGURE 7.3** *A Larger Section of Magnetic Tape*

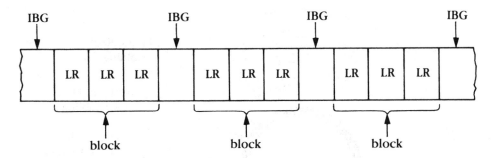

write-protect ring on tape reels. This is a plastic ring that is inserted around the center opening where the reel fits over the spindle. With the ring in place, a notch in the reel is covered, depressing a button on the tape drive when the tape is installed. With the button depressed, the system can write onto the tape. If the ring is not on the reel, the notch is uncovered, allowing the button to remain extended. Under these circumstances the system will reject any request to write data to the tape. This is illustrated in Figure 7.4.

As a closing note, if we know a few pieces of information we can compute the amount of space that a data file will take up on a tape and we can compute the amount of time that will be needed to read and transfer all of the file from tape to some other part of the system. The information we need to do this includes the number of logical records, the length of each logical record (in characters), the blocking factor, the density (in cpi), and the length of the IBGs (in inches). With these numbers, one can determine the amount of tape needed to store a file. This becomes an important consideration when deciding which files to store on which tapes. If we also know the speed at which characters are read and the time it takes to traverse an IBG, we can compute the time needed to read an entire file (not counting the time spent processing the data after it has been read). This may be of concern in studies of system performance and efficiency.

## MAGNETIC DISK

Figure 7.5 shows a surface of a magnetic disk. Note that the data stored on the disk are placed on concentric circles called tracks. Each track goes through several sectors, or pie-shaped wedges. These sectors mark

**FIGURE 7.4**  *Write-Protect Ring*

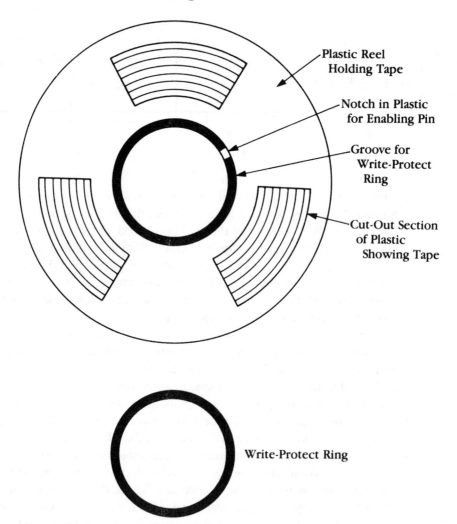

Plastic Reel
Holding Tape

Notch in Plastic
for Enabling Pin

Groove for
Write-Protect
Ring

Cut-Out Section
of Plastic
Showing Tape

Write-Protect Ring

the physical records or blocks on the disk. Notice also that the portion of a track in a sector is shorter for tracks near the center and longer for tracks closer to the edge of the disk. However, because the disk is a solid surface rotating about the center spindle, the time for the portion of a track in a sector to pass under a fixed point is the same, regardless of the track in question. Thus, in most disk systems the amount of data on a track in a sector is constant; the data in the outer tracks are simply less compact than data on the inner tracks. The amount of data that can be stored in such a system is governed by the density of storage on the innermost track.

**FIGURE 7.5** *One Surface of a Disk*

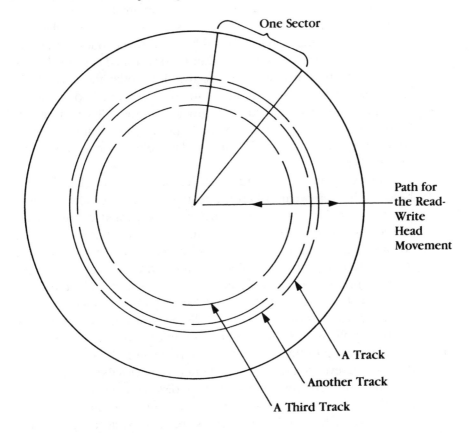

Floating on a very thin cushion of air over the surface of the disk is the read-write head. This cushion of air is between 0.5 microns and 3.0 microns, depending on the density with which data are stored on the disk. (A micron is 0.0001 centimeters, or approximately 0.00004 inches.) On most systems, there is one head that can be moved along a straight line from the outermost track to the innermost track as the disk rotates underneath it. This double motion allows us to have (almost) random access. From any spot on the disk, the system can move fairly quickly to any other spot and does not need to read the data over which it is passing. For this reason, disks are almost always used as the storage medium for files that provide random access (namely, index-sequential and direct organization files). Furthermore, sequential organization files are also stored on disks if they need to be on-line for the system, since disks have become the major devices for secondary storage.

There are two movements involved in moving from one place to another on the disk, and hence two factors in any time delay considerations. The first factor is called the seek time, which is the time needed to move the read-write head from its current track to the track containing the data desired. The other factor is called rotational delay, which is the time needed to rotate the disk under the head to the proper sector for the data. Some of the more expensive disk systems have an entire array of read-write heads over each disk surface, one head for each track. These systems avoid the seek time factor altogether, since changing tracks merely involves the electronic enabling of a different head.

Probably the worst disaster that can happen in a disk system is a head crash. This occurs when the read-write head actually comes in contact with the disk surface. This is accompanied by unpleasant screeching, smoke, and the destruction of all data in the vicinity of the contact area. The most likely cause of a head crash is some form of debris interfering with the cushion of air on which the read-write head floats. Consider the three-micron gap of an "inexpensive" disk system (which is of relatively low density of data): a particle of tobacco smoke may be as large as one micron, or fully one-third the size of the gap. Airborne pollens range in size from ten microns to one hundred microns, many times the size of the gap. A single red blood cell has a diameter of seven to eight microns, better than twice the gap size. Thus, we can see that any contamination of the disk pack environment could be catastrophic. An excellent diagram of this situation can be found on page 77 of R. Kenneth Walter's book, referenced at the end of this chapter. As a side note, this problem does not occur with floppy disk systems, in which the head rests directly on the surface anyway. Of course, any debris on the floppy disk will make the data underneath it inaccessible and may necessitate having to remove and clean the head.

Magnetic disks used on minicomputers and mainframes usually come in packs having several platters, each of which has two surfaces. Each surface will have its own read-write head (or array of heads). Some of these packs are fixed, meaning that the pack is a permanent part of the disk drive unit. Others are removable and may be interchanged as needed. All of the platters are mounted on the same spindle, and they all rotate together. In the movable head systems, all heads are on a common unit and they all move in or out together. Thus if we are accessing track number 6, sector number 2 on one surface, the heads for all the other surfaces are over track 6, sector 2 of their surfaces also. In view of this we identify a cylinder as the set of tracks (one from each surface) at a fixed distance from the center. In storing records from a file, if one track is not enough, most systems will use another track in the same cylinder to continue. In this way there is no seek time needed to read through the file; the system simply enables a different head (on a different surface) to read the next group of records.

## MASS STORAGE

As always, the two secondary storage media we have discussed have advantages and disadvantages. Magnetic tape is inexpensive and easily transported, but slow and not suited for random access. The use of tape also requires the intervention of a human computer operator to install the necessary tape on the tape drive before the program can process it. Magnetic disks are more expensive but provide faster retrieval, provide for random access, and are usually on-line without intervention. In an effort to merge the advantages of these two systems, the idea of mass storage was developed.

In mass storage, data are stored on rolls of tape packaged in cartridges, which are stored in a honeycomb arrangement of bins until the data are needed. When a cartridge is requested by a program, a mechanical device retrieves it from its bin, carries it to the read-write device, and installs it. The program can then access the data on that tape. When the program is finished with that cartridge, the mechanical arm removes it from the read-write device and returns it to its bin. Thus, a large volume of data can be stored on an inexpensive medium and available to the computer system without human intervention. Since each cartridge contains a sequential tape, mass storage is not useful for files requiring random access, and since there is the need for physically installing the cartridge, there will be a delay in program execution not experienced with files on disk.

## MAIN MEMORY

Main memory is a high-speed (and hence high-cost) storage medium. A data item must be in main memory in order for the CPU (central processing unit) to have access to it. Thus, any data item that is stored on a secondary storage device must first be copied to main memory in order for the CPU to utilize it. The accessing of data in main memory by the CPU is purely electronic, and hence quite rapid. The transfer between secondary storage and main memory involves the physical movement of a tape or disk, and hence is much slower.

Access to data in main memory is truly random, since any piece of data can be read into the CPU with no physical movement and no reading or passing over of other data. Communication between the CPU and main memory is all controlled by electronic circuitry; all that must be done to carry out the data transfer is to specify the desired address and enable the read (or write) circuits. Of course, because of the complex circuitry and the limit on the number of addresses the CPU can generate, the size of main memory is much less than the amount of space available on disk or tape, which necessitates the transfer of data between main memory and secondary storage. These transfer times are extremely slow compared to processing times, when the CPU is actually carrying out instructions.

As we mentioned earlier, logical records of our file are grouped together into blocks on the secondary storage media. When data are transferred to main memory, an entire block is transferred. The desired record must then be selected from this block. To accommodate this transfer, main memory is also divided into blocks. Thus, communication between main memory and secondary storage involves an entire block at a time, while communication between main memory and the CPU will be in terms of much smaller pieces of data.

## CACHE MEMORY

In order to increase processing speed, some computer systems have a cache memory installed between main memory and the CPU. The name "cache" comes from the French word for "hidden" and was chosen because users are not aware of its existence. Without going into great detail, the idea of cache memory is to take advantage of the natural grouping of data and instructions needed by the CPU. The frequently used items from main memory are often located close together in any process being executed. When a fetch is made to such an area, the whole block is copied from main memory into cache. Later fetches are very apt to be for items in this copied area, which can be fetched from cache instead of main memory. Because more sophisticated (and more expensive) semiconductor technology is used in manufacturing cache memory, this access should be five to ten times faster than retrieval from main memory. Of course, because of the extra expense, cache memories are limited in size and must employ carefully chosen algorithms for copying areas of main memory in and out of cache as well as for determining whether the requested item is in cache or not.

## I/O PROCESSORS AND FILE I/O OPERATIONS

When the program being executed by the CPU needs another record from a file, there obviously has to be some transfer of data in the system. If the record is not already in main memory, it and the block that contains it must be retrieved from secondary storage and put into main memory. The individual logical record needed by the program must then be copied from its location in the block in main memory to the location of the program variables in main memory. At this point it is available for access by the CPU. If the record is already in the file block area, it merely has to be copied from that main memory location to the variables' location.

The task of directing these data transfers is usually given to an I/O processor. This I/O processor, which is sometimes called a channel, has to locate the record needed by the CPU, move it to the variables' area of main memory, and inform the CPU of the record's location. A schematic diagram is shown in Figure 7.6. The double arrows indicate the paths of actual data transfers, while the single line indicates flow of control signals and address information.

The I/O processor is a CPU in its own right, but it is one that is dedicated to the task of handling I/O operations between main memory and secondary storage devices. As such, it is smaller and less expensive than the main CPU and has a greatly simplified operating system. The

**FIGURE 7.6** *The Role of an I/O Processor*

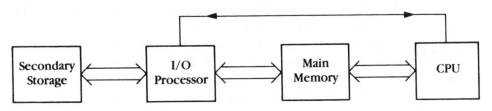

reason to have this structure is to free the main CPU from having to oversee these data transfers. Since these involve the physical movements of the secondary storage devices, they are extremely slow in comparison to internal CPU operations. Rather than have the CPU stand idle while the transfers are taking place, the CPU can turn that task over to the I/O processor and switch to another task while waiting for the data to arrive in the variables area. At this point, the CPU can then switch back to the suspended task and resume its execution.

## EFFICIENCY CONSIDERATIONS

Now that we have discussed the nature of memory and secondary storage and the process of moving data back and forth, we can explain comments made in previous chapters regarding the value of sorting transactions and of holding each master record until all transactions for it are processed. Recall from Chapter 3 that we must sort transactions and hold each master until it is completely finished when updating a sequentially organized file. However, with index-sequential and direct files, sorting and holding are not required. This section will consider the pros and cons of including these features in the updating algorithm, even though they are not essential.

For each master record that the update program is to manipulate there are two possible transfers of data, one from secondary storage to the file block area of main memory and one from the file block area to the variables area. The first transfer moves not only the desired logical record but all the other logical records in the block containing the desired record. This transfer is also much slower because of the physical movements involved with the secondary storage device. The second transfer is purely electronic. Notice that the decision to hold a master record until all transactions for it are completed will reduce the number of transfers within main memory. For example, for a master record having three transactions, our update algorithms (from Chapters 4 and 5) will transfer the record three times in each direction between the file block area and the variables area. If we modify the algorithm to hold the master record until it is finished, the record will only be transferred once in each direction. We thus gain a relatively small savings in transfer time, but we also have a more complicated program to write, test, and debug, and a program with more variables and lines of code to execute. Unless execution speed is extremely critical, the advantages of holding each master record are probably not worth the costs.

In the algorithm to update a file with index-sequential organization, sorting the transactions first can bring about a significant savings in execution time. In most systems, records in an index-sequential file are grouped in blocks by primary key value. If the transactions are sorted and the master records are grouped on the same ordering, we can expect to need each block of records only once. The smallest transaction key will bring that block from secondary storage into main memory and all other master records in that block that need to be updated will be processed by the transactions immediately following. Thus, blocks that have master records to be modified will be fetched once and other blocks will not be fetched at all. We can't expect any more efficient processing than this.

The savings in updating a direct organization file is not quite as clear. Of course, if we are using direct addressing, we have the same efficiency gain as with the index-sequential file. If we have indirect addressing we cannot expect master records with keys that are close together in value to have addresses that are close together, and the possibility of collisions means that we may have to search several blocks anyway. However, if the hashing scheme tends to be locally order preserving and if the number of overflow records is small, having the transactions sorted can bring about the same type of savings as we saw with index-sequential files. Note that the prime division/remainder hashing function is locally order preserving, since increasing the key value by one will increase the home address by one (except at the upper end of the range of home addresses, where increasing the key by one sends you back to the beginning of the range).

Of course, we need to balance the run time saved in the update program against the run time needed to sort the transactions. Whether the sorting is done by an application program or a system utility, there will be a drain on the available time of the system. With the efficient algorithms for sorting that most sort utilities use, it seems reasonable that sorting will be less time-consuming than the extra block transfers in the update process that would result from unsorted transactions. Finally, note that a decision to hold master records requires that the transactions be sorted.

## HANDLING VARIABLE-LENGTH RECORDS

There are two main situations in which we would want to have records in a data file be of different lengths, one at the program level and the other at the secondary storage level. At the storage level, there are apt to be fields defined at a maximum-needed length that will include several characters of blank space in most records. For example, a field for last names should probably be declared as twenty to twenty-five characters long. However, most last names use fifteen or fewer characters. When writing these records to our secondary storage device, it would be more economical to compress out these trailing blank spaces rather than store the repeated ASCII code (or EBCDIC) generated by the space bar on the keyboard. Once this is done, however, the field size of our record description cannot be used to determine where this field stops and the next field begins. Furthermore, the system cannot use the record length to compute the location of the next record in the file for sequential reading.

There are basically two approaches that could be used to deal with the problems mentioned above. First, any potentially varying fields could be prefixed with a system-generated and maintained count of the number of characters actually stored for that field. Thus, when the I/O processor goes to store the record, it will subtract the number of trailing blanks from the declared field size and put this result as a prefix to the field contents before writing the record to secondary storage. When retrieving the record, the I/O processor will examine this prefix and expand the actual data with the necessary number of blanks before sending it to main memory. These counts could also be used (along with declared sizes of nonvarying fields) to calculate the position of the next record in the file. The alternative to a prefixed character count would be to append a special "end-of-field" character after the significant data. This end-of-field marker would be an ASCII code (or EBCDIC) not used for any character that might be included in a data file. Another special code could be used as an end-of-record marker to facilitate jumps to the beginning of the next record in sequence.

The other situation that leads to variable-length records is at the programmer's level, although the programmer is probably not in a position to control the handling of this variability. The situation arises when we have a record design with a "repeating field." Repeating fields occur when a particular type of data item might occur several times for one individual record. For example, in a file of student information, we might want to store the courses in which each student is enrolled. Since students normally take more than one course, this course field would need to be repeated. The problem is that there is no set number of courses that every student must take. A part-time student might have only one course. A full-time student who must take a collection of one-credit courses might have as many as ten. However, it would be quite wasteful to store ten course fields for each record, since the vast majority of students would have far fewer courses. Again, we can either use a prefixed count for the number of copies of this repeating field or some sort of special character to mark the end of the list. Care must be taken to distinguish between counts (or markers) for a single field with trailing blanks removed and counts (or markers) for lists of repeating fields.

There is also a third situation that leads to variable-length records, but it does not occur very often in well-designed data files. This situation involves several record formats within one file. As an example, suppose we wanted to set up a file with data on the people with whom a university deals. The records for faculty would have a different format from those of students, and both of these would be different from the format for businesses supplying goods and services. Each record would have to contain a field identifying its type so that the programs could select the proper routines to process it as well as the proper format for interpreting the data fields. As the example illustrates, records of different formats normally should be put into different files rather than lumped together into one hodgepodge file.

As a final note, we should observe that the space saved by allowing variable-length records must be balanced against the overhead. For example, a field whose values will vary from fifteen to eighteen characters offers little chance for savings, since two characters would be needed for a count (or one for a marker). The extra processing time needed to interpret the varying length in this case probably makes the gain in space insignificant. Likewise, with repeating fields, if all records will have either five or six copies of the field it is probably not worth the bother of using variable-length records. Providing six copies for each record is apt to be better than dealing with the overhead of distinguishing those with five from those with six.

---

## CONCLUDING REMARKS

In this brief overview of computer hardware, we have focused on equipment that would normally come into play in file processing operations, with an eye toward what effect this equipment might have on those operations (in terms of efficiency, for the most part). These issues would normally be of concern to systems analysts and operating system designers rather than to the application programmer. As technology marches on, improvements will naturally be made to these hardware devices and entirely new devices to serve these purposes will be developed. Keeping informed of these developments will provide an interesting challenge for those in computer science and computer operations.

## EXERCISES

**1.** Explain the following in your own words:
  **a.** interblock gap on magnetic tape
  **b.** blocking factor
  **c.** mass storage
  **d.** cache memory
  **e.** I/O processors
  **f.** variable-length records
  **g.** repeating fields

**2.** What gains can we expect from sorting transactions before updating? What are the costs?

**3.** What gains can we expect from holding a master record until all transactions for it are processed? What are the costs?

**4.** What is the formula that would compute the amount of tape needed to store a file? How would this formula be modified to compute disk space?

**5.** What is the formula that would compute the amount of time needed to read a file from tape? How would this formula be modified to compute the time needed to read from disk?

**6.** Why would records of a file be stored on one cylinder of a disk pack instead of on the same disk surface?

**7.** What are the advantages and disadvantages of single-head-per-surface disk drives compared to those that have a head for each track?

**8.** In your own words, explain the two methods of handling compressed fields in variable-length records.

**9.** Explain the two approaches to handling repeated fields in variable-length records.

## OTHER READINGS

**1.**   Claybrook, B. *File Management Techniques* (New York: John Wiley & Sons, 1983), Chapter 2.

**2.**   Smith, A. J. "Cache Memories," *Computing Surveys,* vol. 14, no. 3 (September 1982), pp. 473–530.

**3.**   Walter, R. Kenneth. *Introduction to Data Management and File Design* (Englewood Cliffs, NJ: Prentice-Hall, 1986), Chapters 3 and 4.

# 8 AN OVERVIEW OF DATABASE PROCESSING

In the previous chapters we looked at how data could be structured in a file, how these files could be updated and processed, and how these structures could be implemented with computer hardware and software. In this chapter we will examine some of the problems associated with processing data organized in files and how database processing avoids these problems. This chapter is not intended to give the reader a thorough knowledge of database operations, but it should provide a link between the file processing work of the first seven chapters and the study of database management systems.

## PROBLEMS OF A FILE PROCESSING ENVIRONMENT

Before we actually begin our explanation of database systems, let us develop an example to be used in this chapter for illustrating the concepts to be presented. Assume we are involved in the computer center of a university. The dean of students wants to keep computerized records of all students enrolled in the university; the registrar wants to keep a computer listing of courses being taught; the personnel office needs information on the faculty employed at the university; and, of course, there is a good deal of other data for which the computer center is responsible. The exact nature of the data to be stored is not important right now and will be explained in more detail when it is needed. For now, we will use this example to compare and contrast a file processing environment with a database processing environment.

Suppose that the director of the computer center assigned three different staff members to the three offices mentioned above. Each of these people would meet with the users to whom they had been assigned, analyze the users' situation, and develop a file processing system to meet their needs. This would result in the situation diagrammed in Figure 8.1. This figure shows a setup that at first glance appears to handle the case described above, but which (potentially) has some serious flaws. This kind of situation, by the way, was not uncommon in the earlier days of data processing. We will identify four such flaws, describing each in turn below.

## Data Isolation

With the structure shown in Figure 8.1, it is quite possible to suffer the problems of data isolation. There are related data in the system that we might not be able to bring together. This would be the case if each office felt that it "owned" its data and would not grant permission to anyone else to use it. It would also occur if the three systems had been developed in different programming languages that produced incompatible files, so that no single program could access more than one of the three files. Now suppose that the academic vice president wants to know if any faculty without doctoral degrees are teaching upper-level courses. Information on upper-level courses is in the course file and information on nondoctoral faculty is in the faculty file. All the data needed to answer the question are stored in the computer system, but we can't get it. We would have to list the faculty names in question in one report, the courses in question in another, and then manually check the two reports to match instructor names with courses. The delays involved are not going to help the vice president's opinion of the computer center staff.

## Data Duplication

Since the different systems may need the same data (such as the highest degree earned by a faculty member) and since we might not be able to cross files to get this information, we need to store the data in each file. There are two problems associated with this duplication. First, there is the extra storage space that this requires. Second, there is the matter of inconsistency. If we store the same data item in two places, there is a chance that we will have two different values. For example, suppose that we have faculty degree information in both the course file and the faculty file and that a faculty member has been engaged in further graduate study since being hired. When his or her degree requirements have been completed, we will have to perform two separate update procedures on two separate files to maintain consistency.

**FIGURE 8.1** *A File Processing Environment*

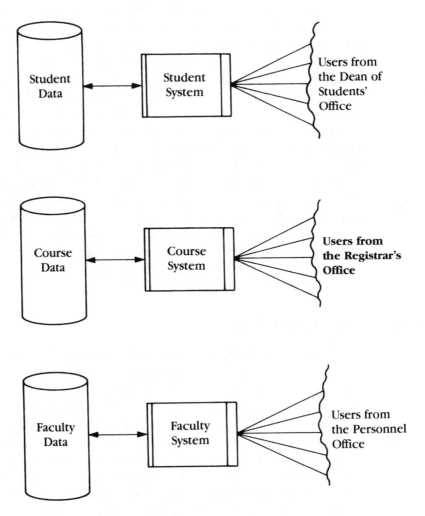

## Program/Data Dependency

In order for a program to make sense of the data in a record from a file, there must be a description of the layout of the record. This description tells what data items are located in the record, where they start and end, and what data type they are. This description is actually a property of the file, but in an application programming/file processing environment, the description is stored in the programs. This is called program/data dependency and it leads to headaches in program maintenance. For example, our student data records would probably contain (in this order) fields for student identification number, student name, home address (broken down into street, city, state, and zip code), and other data such as major and credits completed. Every program using this file must have this layout stored in its code, including the amount of space set aside for zip code. Originally, zip codes were composed of five digits, but now the post office has begun to use nine-digit zip codes. As this change is made, all records in the file will have to be expanded and the other data will have to be moved to the right in the layout. A program that merely identifies seniors according to the number of credits completed should not be affected by this change, since it does not care about zip codes, but the location of the data it needs would now be different. So this program will have to be edited, recompiled, and retested, as will all the other programs that use the student file. Identifying all such programs and then modifying, recompiling, and retesting them is apt to be a very extensive job, which would be unnecessary if the record descriptions were where they really belong—with the data file instead of the program.

## Program Development Time

As you have most likely noticed (assuming that you have done some programming assignments from the previous chapters), writing, testing, and debugging programs in a file processing environment can be a lengthy and time-consuming activity. It has been said that a backlog of two years is not uncommon in data processing centers. Assuming that projects are begun in the order they are received, a vice president who requests a new report would have to wait two years before getting that report. A two-year backlog in data processing is similar to a two-year backlog in a maternity ward. If you have to wait that long, you'll find another way to deal with the situation. Again, this does not improve the vice president's opinion of the data processing center.

   In all fairness to the file processing environment, it must be said that recent software products (called file management systems, or FMS) have alleviated some of these problems. For example, with these file management systems we no longer have to worry about data isolation because all files produced by the system are compatible. The discussion above describes the situation in the 1960s when database systems began to emerge, mainly to cope with the four problems mentioned. It wasn't until the late 1970s that file management systems began to appear on the market.

# DEFINITION OF THE DATABASE PROCESSING ENVIRONMENT

Figure 8.2 shows the same data processing situation as Figure 8.1, but with the use of a database system instead of a file processing system. Notice that all the data files are collected into one structure called the database, illustrated by the rectangular box in the figure. Included in the database is also the data dictionary, which is a system-generated file (or files) of data descriptions and related information. The data files, since they are in the same structure, are completely compatible. In fact, the system is "expecting" them to be used in combinations instead of singly. This organization immediately solves the first three problems listed above. Since all files are fully compatible, there is no data isolation. Since files are all accessible, we do not need to duplicate data; we can simply access another file if the data we need are not in the file we are currently using. Because of the data dictionary, the program/data dependency problem is removed. We will come back to the issue of program development time shortly. All in all, it looks like

**FIGURE 8.2**  *A Database Environment*

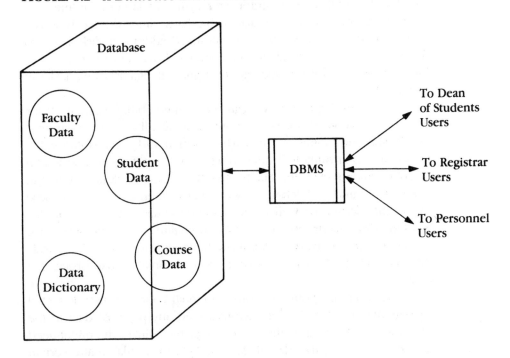

a pretty good situation. With this much of a description, we can now define a database (as Kroenke and Dolan have done in *Database Processing*) to be an integrated, self-describing collection of files.

There is an additional system box in the diagram, labeled DBMS. This stands for database management system, which is a software product used to manage the database. On further examination, we see some drawbacks and potential problems with database processing. First, the tasks performed by a DBMS are quite complicated and function at a level somewhat similar to an operating system. Thus, it is not reasonable to expect that these products can be produced in-house in a data processing center, and they tend to be expensive when purchased from a vendor. Without naming names, a typical DBMS for a typical minicomputer had a list price of approximately $60,000 in 1990. In the past, some database management systems have sold for as much as half a million dollars. Of course, there are database management systems available for single-user microcomputer systems that list for less than $500, and clones are available through catalogs for under $100. But in any case, the decision to use database processing will require an expenditure for the purchase of the software to manage the database. Not apparent from the diagram, but still an issue, is the possible need for hardware expansion to support the database and DBMS. Since the DBMS is a complicated program, we may need a larger main memory to keep response time at an acceptable level. Since the database is a more complicated structure, we may need additional disk space to handle the extra overhead without compromising performance. These hidden costs must be worked into the arguments against using database processing.

Also from Figure 8.2, we can see a vulnerability problem. If for any reason the DBMS becomes nonfunctional, all data processing for the database will come to a halt. This problem did not exist in the file processing environment. Notice in Figure 8.1 that if the course system becomes inoperative, the faculty system and the student system can continue to function. Of course, with a well-written DBMS (and at these prices they *should* be well written), the only reason this vulnerability should become a problem is a hardware malfunction in the disk drive containing this software. Such an equipment failure would severely hamper operations regardless of the organization of the data processing systems.

Our diagram points to some potential concerns also. It would appear that any user could have access to any piece of data in the database. A work-study student in the registrar's office who might need to examine the course data to see if a room is available at a certain time for a special meeting should not be allowed to look at student grades. The problem of selective access to the database for different users is called security, and if the DBMS does not provide it we will have problems with unauthorized data access.

There is also a concern with concurrency control. Since the data are shared, there is a possibility that two users may try to modify the same data at more or less the same time. Remember that the actual database resides on disk and that the CPU can only manipulate data in main memory. Suppose that a student has taken summer school courses at two other institutions and we are going to add these transfer credits to the student's record. Since the notifications are coming from two sources, it is possible that two different clerks are entering the changes at more or less the same time. Further, let's suppose that the student previously had forty-two credits, and earned three credits at one school and six credits at the other. Thus, after the updates, the student should have fifty-one credits. Suppose that clerk A enters the request to add six credits, the CPU retrieves the current number of credits (forty-two) from the database, adds six (to make forty-eight), and then is suspended. Suppose then that clerk B's request to add three credits is initiated, the CPU retrieves the current value from the disk file for the database (still forty-two) and adds three (making forty-five) before being suspended. Control could then return to clerk A's request, which writes its value (forty-eight) into the database and terminates. Clerk B's request is then resumed, and write its value (forty-five) into the database. Thus, according to the database we started with forty-two, added nine, and got forty-five. Obviously, the DBMS has to be written so that this type of situation cannot occur.

---

## PROCEDURAL VERSUS NON-PROCEDURAL LANGUAGES

Whether we are working in a database environment or not, there must be some language in which we are communicating with the computer system. In the previous chapters, we have been considering programming languages (such as BASIC, FORTRAN, COBOL, or Pascal). These languages are procedural, because the programmer must describe in some detail all the steps necessary for the completion of the task. For example, to average the credits earned by CS majors in the student file, a program would have to explicitly set the sum and count to zero, read the first record, then iterate until all records have been read. Within each pass of the iteration, the program code would check the major field of the current record, then add one to the count and add the credits to the sum if the major is CS, then read the next record to set up the next iteration pass. When the end of the file is reached, the program code would call for the sum to be divided by the count (after ascertaining that the count was not still zero) and display the result. This detailed explanation of how to accomplish the task is what makes the language in which this program was written procedural.

If, on the other hand, we do not need to specify the process in our code but need only indicate the result to be produced, we are dealing with a non-procedural language. The averaging example explained in the last paragraph becomes something to the effect of "find the average of credits for all CS majors." Two things should be obvious here. First, programs in a non-procedural language are much faster and easier to design, code, and test than are programs in a procedural language. The newer database systems (the relational products discussed below) have these non-procedural languages incorporated and therefore avoid the fourth problem mentioned in the discussion of file processing environmemts. Second, these detailed procedures somehow have to be worked out and executed. In a non-procedural language, this is done by the software rather than by the user.

To give you a better understanding of procedural versus non-procedural languages, consider the task of listing the names and departments of faculty without doctoral degrees who are teaching courses at or above the 300 level, which was mentioned in the discussion of data isolation in a previous section. A procedural language program might be written to iterate through the faculty file and check each faculty member's degree. For any faculty without a doctorate, the courses file would be searched for courses that person is teaching. If the course number is 300 or higher, the faculty member's name and department are printed. The program code would have to have the detailed commands for the main iteration on faculty records, plus the code for the inner iteration on an instructor's courses, along with the checking and printing operations.

Let us now consider an SQL "program" to produce the same result. SQL was developed by IBM as part of their relational database product line, and its form and syntax are currently used in relational database products from a number of other software companies. This code (shown in Figure 8.3) assumes that the faculty records contain fields Name, Department, and Degree (among others), and that course records contain fields for Course_Number and Instructor. The SELECT statement identifies the type of data to be returned, the FROM clause indicates the sources of this data, and the WHERE clause tells the system what restrictions describe the data we want. As you can see, the SQL is extremely short and fairly straightforward. The two-year backlog in developing application programs seems avoidable with the use of such non-procedural languages.

**FIGURE 8.3  *An SQL Example***

```
SELECT NAME, DEPARTMENT
FROM FACULTY, COURSES
WHERE NAME = INSTRUCTOR
        AND DEGREE <> DOCTORATE
        AND COURSE_NUMBER >= 300
```

Another non-procedural "language" used with some relational database products is called QBE (for Query-by-Example), also developed by IBM. In this approach, the user is presented with a blank template of the needed data records and fills in the required values. The system then finds the desired data and displays them for the user. The QBE solution to the problem above is given in Figure 8.4. In this figure, the P. indicates what is to be printed and the _x and _y are variable names. Again, we see that the user does not have to be concerned at all with the process of getting this information, just with describing the information desired.

**FIGURE 8.4  *A QBE Example***

| Faculty | Name | Department | Degree | ••• |
|---------|------|------------|--------|-----|
|  | P._x | P._y | < > DOCTORAL |  |

| Courses | Number | Instructor | ••• |
|---------|--------|------------|-----|
|  | > = 300 | _x |  |

---

# MAJOR TYPES OF DATABASE MANAGEMENT SYSTEMS

There are three major types of database management systems: hierarchy, network (or CODASYL), and relational. We will present them (briefly) in the order of their historical development. Realize, of course, that the presentation here is not complete, but is intended merely to give a general overview.

The first database management systems were of the hierarchy model and began to be developed in the early 1960s. In this model, data are stored in record types and relationships between data are expressed by pointers, or links. Thus, for the example presented above, we would have a record type for faculty data, a record type for course data, and so on. There is a one-to-many relationship between faculty and courses, since one faculty member may teach several courses, but a course is only taught by one faculty member (assuming that we do not wish to allow team teaching). Hence we will have a link between the faculty record type and the course record type, and this link structure will connect faculty records to course records based on the teaching assignments. These links can be traversed in either direction.

The organization of the database can be represented in a data structure diagram (or DSD), with each record type pictured as a rectangle and each link as a line between the record types it is connecting. These lines have a single arrowhead at the "one" side of the relationship and two arrowheads at the "many" side. The DSD for our partial database is shown in Figure 8.5. The main restriction in the hierarchy model can be explained as follows: In the data structure diagram of the database, a record type may have only one parent. In other words,

**FIGURE 8.5  *A Partial DSD***

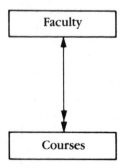

a record can be on the "many" side of only one relationship in the database. If we had a record type for classrooms, we would have a one-to-many relationship between rooms and courses, since each room could have several courses assigned to it (meeting at different times), but a course would be assigned to only one room. This is shown in Figure 8.6. The fact that this situation cannot be handled directly in the hierarchy model meant that some unnatural twists had to be added, making these database systems somewhat less useful. We will not take the time to explain how the hierarchy products solved this problem, since they are seldom used any more.

During the late 1960s, the people involved in CODASYL (which stands for Committee On DAta SYstems Languages) set up a database task group (DBTG) that formulated the network model. This model is frequently referred to as the CODASYL DBTG model. It is extremely similar to the older hierarchy model but it allows a record type to have more than one parent record type. Thus the DSD of Figure 8.6 (which could not be handled directly in the hierarchical model) would be a legal organization in the network model. Several commercial database management systems were based on this model and are still in use at a number of installations.

In 1970, work was begun on the relational model. In this approach, data are stored in tabular form and relationships are expressed by matching data values. The SQL example in Figure 8.3 and the QBE example in Figure 8.4 are both based on the relational model, and the connection between faculty and courses that we needed was expressed by having the same value for the course instructor as for the faculty name. This model was developed in a rigorous manner, based on relations and set theory. Almost all newer database management system

**FIGURE 8.6** *A DSD Not Allowed in the Hierarchy Model*

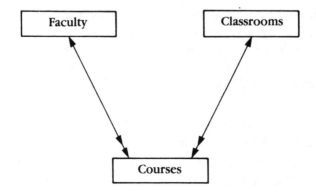

products are relational, including most DBMS products for microcomputers. Furthermore, a number of network products have written relational "front ends," so that users of the database see relational-type commands and structures even though the database is stored internally as a network.

In our survey of these three models we have discussed the concept of the one-to-many relationship and the different ways to handle it. However, there are situations that are many-to-many. For example, each student may enroll in several courses, and we would hope that each course would have several students. Thus there is a many-to-many relationship between courses and students. At present, this situation is handled by creating what is called an intersection record. In this case the intersection record type could be labeled "enrollment." An enrollment record will identify a student and a course that the student is taking. If a student is taking five courses, there will be five enrollment records for that student. If a course has twenty-seven students, it will have twenty-seven enrollment records attached to it. There is a one-to-many relationship between students and enrollment records, and another one-to-many relationship between courses and enrollment records. This is fine for the relational and the network models, but it violates the restriction of the hierarchy model. This may seem like extra fuss and bother, but frequently there are data associated with a many-to-many relationship. In this example, that data would include the grade the student earned in the course. The grade is rather meaningless unless you know both the student and the course involved.

## THE MAIN FUNCTIONS OF A DBMS

In his Turing award lecture in 1981, E. F. Codd identified eight functions that a database management system should be able to do. In this section, we will consider each of these functions briefly, and add a ninth function to his list. A course in database management would consider how these functions might actually be implemented in a DBMS software package.

*1.*  The DBMS, obviously, should be able to store, retrieve, and update the data in the database.

*2.*  The DBMS should provide a user-accessible catalog of data in the database. Recall that a database was defined as being self-describing. This catalog (or data dictionary) contains all the naming and formatting information regarding the structure of the database, and the database system should provide commands by which the user can see this information.

**3.** The DBMS should allow for the declaration and enforcement of logical transactions. A logical transaction is a collection of database commands (or operations) that represent a single real-world action. For example, suppose a student wishes to change sections of a course. The single real-world action requires that the enrollment record be modified and that each of the class size fields in the course records be adjusted by decreasing the count in the dropped section and increasing the count in the added section. All three database changes must be made to represent the selection change. The DBMS should provide a means of collecting all three database updates into a single unit and of ensuring that if the unit is interrupted (by a power failure, for example) the portion that was executed is undone. In other words, either all of a logical transaction is performed or none of it is performed.

**4.** The DBMS should be able to recover from failure. Any number of things can go wrong: the power can go out because a truck ran into the poles carrying the electrical lines; someone can trip over the cord from the computer and pull it out of the socket; the program controlling the transaction might have a bug in it; the transaction request may call for nonexistent data records. Murphy's law says that at the worst possible time something will go wrong. The DBMS must be able to restore the database to a correct state, perhaps requiring some transactions to be resubmitted.

**5.** The DBMS must be able to control concurrent processing, at least in a multiuser system. This was one of the more pressing concerns mentioned in a previous section. Of course, if we are operating on a single-user microcomputer, there is no opportunity for concurrent processing, so we don't need to control it.

**6.** The DBMS should provide a means for enforcing security. Again, this was a concern raised earlier. We must be able to declare who should have what access to which data and the DBMS should then provide that access and no more. Notice that this is a concern on any system. The fact that only one user is allowed on at a time does not mean that only one person will ever use the data. Even on a microcomputer, the DBMS must be able to identify each user and allow only the designated access for that user.

**7.**    The DBMS should be able to interface with the computer system's data communications software, especially in situations involving networking of workstations.

**8.**    There should be facilities to enforce the integrity constraints on the database. For example, if course numbers are to be between 100 and 499, the database should reject any request to create a course number outside this range. If only upper-class students can enroll in 300- or 400-level courses, the database should reject requests to enroll an under-class student in an upper-level course.

**9.**    The DBMS should provide some basic utilities to facilitate operations. These might include modules for backup and restoration of the data or for loading large sets of records into the database files.

## THE ROLE OF THE DBA

In any organization using a database system, there must be a person or group of people in charge of the database operations. This individual or group is called the database administrator, or DBA. The DBA is responsible for assisting users in the design and implementation of their databases and for training them in the processing of their data. The DBA is expected to oversee the performance of the hardware and software involved in the database processing. Finally, the most demanding (and rewarding) aspect of the DBA's work is to referee disputes between users with conflicting objectives and arrive at compromises that are in the best overall interests of the organization. This position requires a good deal of technical expertise as well as the ability to deal effectively with other people, both as a consultant and as a mediator. Because of these demands, the position is a high-priced career option for those who have the knowledge and the personality to carry through with it.

## CONCLUDING REMARKS

This chapter has presented a quick overview of the area of database processing as an alternative to (or an extension of) file processing. We have seen both the advantages and costs/problems associated with database operations, and gained some insight into what database systems should actually be able to do. There is a very real sense that database processing might well replace the vast majority of file processing operations in the not-too-distant future. Of course, database systems are in essence an extra layer on top of the file processing structures that we have discussed. Any DBMS must provide, or have access to, the file manipulation features previously discussed. By the same token, the database systems of the near future will be even more powerful and user-friendly. As hardware and software improve, we will see more of such things as hyper-text and distributed databases. We can expect that more and more data processing activities will be founded in database systems.

---

## EXERCISES

1. In your own words, compare the file processing environment with the database environment. Indicate the advantages and disadvantages (or concerns) with database processing.

2. Explain the difference between procedural and non-procedural languages.

3. What is the distinction between the network model and the hierarchy model for database systems? Which is more useful?

4. List and explain the major functions that a database management system should be able to perform.

5. Explain the job of the DBA, the background that a person should have before accepting this position, and the reason that such a background is important.

---

## OTHER READINGS

1. Codd, E. F. "A Relational Model of Data for Large Shared Data Banks," *Communications of the ACM,* vol. 13, no. 7 (June 1970), p. 337.

2. Codd, E. F. "Relational Database: A Practical Foundation for Productivity" (the 1981 Turing Award Lecture), *Communications of the ACM,* vol. 25, no. 2 (February 1982), p. 109.

**3.** Date, C. J. *An Introduction to Database Systems,* vols. 1 (3d ed.) and 2 (Reading, MA: Addison-Wesley Publishing Co., 1981 and 1982).

**4.** Kroenke, David, and Dolan, Kathleen. *Database Processing,* 3d ed. (Chicago: Science Research Associates, 1988).

# 9 MERGING AND SORTING

We have focused in this book on the updating aspect of file maintenance. In this chapter we will consider two other types of file maintenance. In the first section, we will consider the problem of putting two sorted files together into one file so that the resultant file will also be sorted. Sorted here means that the records are in order according to their primary key values. After that, we will consider the problem of taking an unsorted file and getting it into sorted order. In looking at this, we will review techniques of sorting that can be used on arrays of data stored in main memory, then move to the sorting of files located in secondary storage. We will conclude our discussion with a brief overview of the issue of efficiency of sorting techniques.

## MERGING TWO FILES

There are occasions where it becomes necessary to take two (or more) sequentially organized files that have the same record format and combine them into one file. If the two original files are in order by some field value and if we wish to preserve this ordering in the combined filed, we need to perform a merge operation, which will be explained below. As examples of situations where merging is needed, first suppose that each department in a corporation maintains the data on its own employees, but does so in a companywide standard format and in alphabetical order by name. If the corporation wants to generate a single (alphabetical) listing of all its employees, these files have to be merged together. Second, suppose that we have several faculty members recording the names of students who are adding and dropping courses. These lists (once they are properly ordered) need to be merged (according to that ordering) to provide an overall record of add/drop activity. The idea of merging will also play a role in the sorting of a large data file, which will be discussed in a later section of this chapter.

**143**

The basic idea in merging two files is to get the first record from each file and then iterate the process of comparing the two records, sending the "smaller" record to the new (merged) file and replacing the record sent with the next record from the corresponding input file. This will continue until one of the files is exhausted, at which point we move all remaining records from the other file to the output file. The algorithm is shown in detail below. In the algorithm, the two files are identified as file-A and file-B. The corresponding records and sort fields are record-A, record-B, field-A, and field-B. The algorithm assumes that the end-of-file flags used to terminate the iterations are set only inside the read modules. Again, as was discussed in Chapter 3, whether the end-of-file condition is checked before or after the read command is issued depends on the programming language being used. The algorithm here checks the status of the file first.

### *Merge file–A and file–B*

```
open file-A
open file-B
set flags and counters
Read-A
Read-B
until (end-of-file-A) or (end-of-file-B)
      Select-and-Pass
if (end-of-A)
    then Finish-B
    else Finish-A
close file-A
close file-B
display summary information
```

### *Read–A*

```
if not (end-of-A)
    then read record-A
    else set flag for end-of-A
```

### *Read–B*

```
if not (end-of-B)
    then read record-B
    else set flag for end-of-B
```

### Select–and–Pass

```
if field-A < field-B
    then write record-A
        Read-A
    else if field-A > field-B
        then write record-B
            Read-B
        else handle duplicate field values
```

### Finish–A

```
until (end-of-A flag is turned on)
    write record-A
    Read-A
```

### Finish–B

```
until (end-of-B flag is turned on)
    write record-B
    Read-B
```

A couple of closing observations about this merging are in order here. First, in the Select-and-Pass module, notice the last line, which calls for handling duplicates. The processing to be done if the values from the two files are identical depends on the nature of the situation. In some cases it may be appropriate to omit both record-A and record-B from the new file with an update error message. It might be reasonable to include one of these records and omit the other. It might even be proper to include both records. It all depends on the specifications of the user.

Second, the algorithm is set up to handle values in order from smallest to largest, which is referred to as increasing order. We will assume that all orderings discussed in this chapter are increasing. If a decreasing ordering is desired, the algorithms must be modified, but only by reversing the directions of the inequalities in the data value comparison tests.

A third observation is that the merge process is very similar to the updating of a sequential file, except that the transaction file may only contain add requests and we blur the distinction between the master and transaction files.

## INTERNAL SORTING

In this section, we will consider five algorithms for *in situ* sorting. This requires that the set of data to be sorted is small enough so that it will all fit in the computer's main memory at the same time (usually in an array-type structure) and that the sorting is to be done without creating a second copy of the structure. In other words, we will assume that the data are in a main-memory array and that the sorting is to be done by interchanging elements within the array rather than by creating a second array to hold copies of the data items in their proper order. As was mentioned above, we are assuming that sorted data are to be in increasing order in these algorithms, realizing that decreasing order can be attained (if desired) with only minor modification to the algorithms. We will refer to the array holding the data as A in our pseudocode, and $j$ and $k$ will be used as indices into the array. The number of items in the array to be sorted is identified as $n$. We will also tacitly assume that no duplication of the values used in the sorting decision can occur (for example, if we are sorting student records by name, we are not expecting duplicate names to occur). Extra code may need to be added to the algorithms if such duplication might occur or if some action or further decision as to ordering are desired.

### Insertion Sort

In an insertion sort, the data in the first part of the array are in proper order relative to each other and the remaining part is unchecked (and therefore assumed to be unsorted). We begin by realizing that the first element, taken by itself, must be in the proper order relative to itself. We then iterate, extending the length of the first (sorted) part of the array and thus decreasing the length of the second (unsorted) part of the array. In this iteration, an insertion sort takes the next item in the array (that is, the first element of the second part) and works it into its proper place relative to the data in the first part of the array. In other words, if the data in positions 1 through 5 are in their correct relative order, the next pass through the iteration will look at the data item in position number 6 and insert it in its proper place relative to the five items already sorted. When this is accomplished, the data in positions 1 through 6 are in proper sequence and the unsorted portion of the array now starts with position 7.

In linear insertion, we find the location at which to insert the new item by a linear probing, starting with the end of the sorted part and working down toward position number 1. Once we have found the proper location for the new item, all larger items will move up one position and the new item will be put into the resulting gap. To illustrate, let us suppose that the new item is in position 12 as we begin the pass through the iteration loop. We start our linear probing with position 11, looking for an item that is smaller than our new item. If position 11 fails this test, we check position 10, then position 9, and so on until we either find a smaller item or have checked all the way to the first position without success. Let us suppose further that the first smaller item was found in position 3. We put the new item into a temporary variable, then move each item in slots 4 through 11 up one position (actually starting with 11 and working down to 4), and finally put the new item (saved for us in the temporary variable) into position number 4. Now we have slots 1 through 12 in sorted order. Notice that while the first part of the array is in the proper order, the elements in this part of the array are not necessarily in their final position until the algorithm finishes. On each pass of the iteration, any item in the first part might have to move up a position to make way for a new (smaller) item to be inserted.

We now present the full algorithm for the linear insertion sort, followed by a tracing of the algorithm on a sample array.

### The Algorithm for Linear Insertion Sorting

```
for all values of k running from 1 up to n - 1
   new-item  <-- A (k + 1)
   found  <-- false
   j  <-- k
   until (spot is found) or (j = 0)
      if  A (j)  <  new-item
          then found  <--  true
          else j  <--  j - 1
   new-spot  <--  j + 1
   for all values of j from k down to new-spot
      A (j + 1)  <--  A (j)
   A (new-spot)  <--  new-item
```

### A Trace of the Algorithm

```
original data:        8 2 5 7 3    (n = 5)

k = 1:    new-item is A (2), which is 2
          j starts at 1
          A (1) is not less than new-item, j becomes 0
          new-spot is 1
          the 8 in position 1 moves to position 2
          2 is put into position 1
          the list is now     2 8 5 7 3
```

```
k = 2:      new-item is A (3), which is 5
      j starts at 2
      A (2) is not less than new-item, j becomes 1
      A (1) is less than new-item
      new-spot is 2
      the 8 in position 2 moves to position 3
      5 is put into position 2
      the list is now    2  5  8  7  3


k = 3:      new-item is 7
      j starts at 3
      A (3) is not less than new-item, j becomes 2
      A (2) is less than new-item
      new-spot is 3
      the 8 in position 3 moves to position 4
      7 is put into position 3
      the list is now    2  5  7  8  3


k = 4:      new-item is 3
      j starts at 4
      A (4) is not less than new-item, j becomes 3
      A (3) is not less than new-item, j becomes 2
      A (2) is not less than new-item, j becomes 1
      A (1) is less than new-item
      new-spot is 2
      the 8 in position 4 moves to position 5
      the 7 in position 3 moves to position 4
      the 5 in position 2 moves to position 3
      3 is put into position 2
      the list is    2  3  5  7  8 which is sorted
```

The other type of insertion sort to be considered here is called binary insertion. This algorithm is quite similar to linear insertion, except that a binary search (rather than a linear search) is used to locate the proper position for the new item. In a binary search, the interval to be checked is divided in half (as nearly as possible, anyway) and the value in the middle is examined. If the new item is smaller than the middle value, the lower half is considered next; otherwise, the upper half is considered. At each stage, one half of the remaining interval is considered and the other half is ignored. This continues until the interval to be checked has only one element. At this point, the new item either belongs just before or just after this value. The search part of the algorithm is given here. The other part of the algorithm (moving the data around) is the same as for linear insertion. You will recall that "trunc" finds the integer part of a number, so that trunc (7) = 7, while trunc (4.5) = 4.

### *The Algorithm Modification for Binary Insertion*

```
first   <--   1
last    <--   k
until   first = last
    mid   <--   trunc ((first + last)/2)
    if   new-item < A (mid)
        then last <-- larger of (mid - 1, first)
        else first   <--   mid + 1
if new-item < A (first)
    then   new-spot   <--   first
    else   new-spot   <--   first + 1
```

To quickly trace this new portion of the algorithm, let us consider the list a b c e f g h i j k l d, and let us assume that the algorithm is finished with the first eleven positions. Our new item is then the letter d in the twelfth position. To locate the proper position for d, consider the list from positions 1 to 11. Its mid position is trunc ((1 + 11)/2), which is 6. The sixth letter is g, which is larger than the new value. Thus, we now consider the list from positions 1 to 5 (noting that d cannot belong in position 6 or higher, since it has a smaller value than the value in position 6). The midpoint of this interval is 3 and A (3) is less than the new value, so our interval is now from 4 to 5. Its mid position is 4, and A (4) is larger than the new value, leaving us with the "interval" from 4 to 4. Since d is smaller than A (4), the proper location for d is 4, so the letters in 5 through 11 each move up one, and d is inserted into position 4.

In typical situations, a binary search is quicker than a linear search. In a linear search, we can expect, on the average, to have to check half of the items in the list. So in searching lists of $k$ items with a linear search, we can expect to get an average of $k/2$ comparisons per search. In a binary search, we eliminate half of the remaining items from consideration at each step, so the number of comparisons needed is the integer part of the $\log_2 (k)$ to isolate a single element plus one more comparison to decide on which side of that element to put the new item. Of course, we might get lucky in a linear probe and find the spot on the first comparison, but this is unusual and will not pay off unless the data were fairly well sorted before we began. The binary search will not vary much from the $\log_2 (k)$ number of comparisons, regardless of the actual arrangement of the data.

## Shell Sort

The Shell sort was developed by D. L. Shell in 1952 to provide a faster means of sorting than the linear (or binary) insertion algorithm. The basic idea is to note that linear insertion works quite well if the data are already close to being in order. That is, if each new item does not have to be compared with more than a few of the previously handled items, linear insertion works rather quickly. To exploit this observation, the Shell sort begins by breaking the array to be sorted into $k$ parts, each part having approximately $n/k$ elements. Each part is then sorted independently of the other parts by linear insertion. The value of $k$ is then decreased (hence the name "diminishing increments" for this sort) and the resulting parts of the array are again sorted independently via linear insertion. Each part of the array contains elements that are evenly spaced across the array, with the spacing being the value of $k$.

As an example, suppose that $k = 8$ and $n = 20$. Then the first part would contain the elements in positions 1, 9, and 17. An insertion sort would be performed using just these three items. The second part of the array would consist of elements in positions 2, 10, and 18, and these three would be put into the proper order relative to each other. The third part would involve positions 3, 11, and 19, while the fourth part would use items in positions 4, 12, and 20. Each part after this would have only two elements and each pair would be eight positions apart. When each of these eight parts had been sorted (separately from the other parts), the value of $k$ would be reduced. This would determine a smaller number of parts, each having more elements. When $k$ reaches 1, we conclude by performing a regular linear insertion sort, but with the advantage of having the data nearly in order already.

There are a number of algorithms for selecting the values of $k$ to be used in this process, as can be seen by checking various other textbooks. Perhaps the easiest one to implement is to cut the value in half each time. In other words, we take the integer part of $n/2$ as the initial value of $k$. On each successive round, we use the integer part of $k/2$ as the next value of $k$. When the process reaches the point where $k = 1$, the data in the array will be in proper order. Another approach requires that the values of $k$ be chosen so that there are no common divisors between the new value of $k$ and the previous value of $k$. For example, if $n = 20$, we could use 9 as the first value of $k$, since no number (other than 1) divides evenly into both 9 and 20. The second value for $k$ could not be 3 or 6, but could be any other number less than 9. Either 4 or 5 would probably be a good choice here.

## Selection Sort

A straight selection sort is similar to an insertion sort in that we still deal with situations where the first part of the array is in order while the rest of the array is unchecked and assumed to be unsorted. The difference is that with straight selection sorting, we scan the second part of the array to locate the next item to include in the sorted part, rather than simply taking the item in the next position. To be more concrete, suppose that our array has forty-five elements and that positions 1 through 15 have been sorted already. The insertion sorts discussed above would take item number 16 without considering the data in positions 17 to 45. The straight selection sort would examine the data in positions 16 to 45 and select the minimum value. This minimum value would be interchanged with the data item in position 16 to increase the length of the sorted part and thus decrease the length of the unsorted part.

By always selecting the smallest remaining item from the unsorted part of the array for inclusion in the sorted part, we can see that the data items in the sorted part are not only in order relative to themselves but are in fact in their final positions in the fully sorted array. In other words, once the selection of the item to place into position 16 is made, that data item will never have to move out of position 16. Of course, the sorted part must be empty when we start, whereas insertion sorts start with position 1 being "sorted." Below are the algorithm for straight selection sorting and a trace of the algorithm on the data list we used to illustrate linear insertion. Again, A is the array containing the data to be sorted, $n$ is the number of items in the array, and $j$ and $k$ are indices for the array.

### *The Algorithm for Straight Selection Sorting*

```
For all values of k running from 0 to (n - 2)

    min-spot   <--   k + 1
    min-value  <--   A (min-spot)

    For  j  running from (k + 2) to n
         if   A (j) < min-value
              then   min-spot   <--   j
                     min-value  <--   A (j)

    if min-spot > (k + 1)
       then temp    <--   A (min-spot)
            A (min-spot)   <--   A (k + 1)
            A (k + 1)   <--   temp
```

### *A Trace of the Algorithm*

```
original data:    8  2  5  7  3      (n = 5)

k = 0: scanning 1 - 5 gives min-spot = 2,
                             min-value = 2
       switching spots 1 and 2 gives
                                 2  8  5  7  3

k = 1: scanning 2 - 5 gives min-spot = 5,
                             min-value = 3
       switching spots 2 and 5 gives
                                 2  3  5  7  8

k = 2: scanning 3 - 5 gives min-spot = 3,
                             min-value = 5
       since min-spot = k + 1, no switch needed

k = 3: scanning 4 - 5 gives min-spot = 4
       since min-spot = k + 1, no switch needed
```

The list is now known to be sorted.

## Bubble Sort

The bubble sort is something of a hybrid between the insertion sort and the selection sort. It is similar to selection in that the sorted part of the list contains elements that are in their final positions and thus do not need to be considered further. This is achieved, of course, by selecting the proper element from the unsorted portion of the array to append to the sorted part of the array at each step. It is similar to insertion sorting in that the next element to append is chosen not by merely scanning the remaining items but rather by pairwise comparisons and swapping. The bubble sort can be made more efficient by including a test to see if the data are sorted before all passes are made, which would allow for an earlier exit than might be expected. (Notice that in the trace of the selection sort above, the array was actually sorted after the iteration with $k = 1$. The passes for $k = 2$ and $k = 3$ were unnecessary, but there was no way of testing for this without significant addition to the algorithm.) The algorithm and a trace are shown here.

### The Algorithm for the Bubble Sort

```
k    <--   1
repeat
     swap   <--   false

     for  j  running from  n  down to  k + 1
          if      A (j)    <     A (j - 1)
                  then   swap   <--   true
                         temp   <--   A (j - 1)
                         A (j - 1)   <--   A (j)
                         A (j)   <--   temp

     k   <--   k + 1
as long as (k < n) and (swap is true)
```

### A Trace of the Bubble Sort

```
original data:       8  2  5  7  3          (n = 5)

k = 1,   j = 5:      8  2  5  3  7   (swap true)
         j = 4:      8  2  3  5  7
         j = 3:      8  2  3  5  7
         j = 2:      2  8  3  5  7

k = 2,   j = 5:      no swap
         j = 4:      no swap
         j = 3:      2  3  8  5  7   (swap true)

k = 3,   j = 5:      no swap
         j = 4:      2  3  5  8  7   (swap true)

k = 4,   j = 5:      2  3  5  7  8   (swap true)
```

The list is now in proper order.

## Quicksort

Quicksort is an example of a recursive sorting algorithm. The idea of quicksort is to select one value from the list to be sorted (called the pivot), use this value to split the list into two segments, and then invoke quicksort on each segment. While there are a number of variations on how to select a pivot, we will use one of the easiest for our algorithm. So, given a list of values to sort, pick the first one as the pivot. By means to be discussed shortly, rearrange the array so that, if the pivot value is in position $j$, all items in positions up to $j - 1$ are smaller than the pivot and all items in positions $j + 1$ and above are at least as large as the pivot. Then invoke quicksort on the two sublists separated by position $j$.

The rearrangement of the array can be accomplished by using two indices to the array, called LEFT and RIGHT. LEFT should start at the second position of the array while RIGHT starts at the last position, so as we start we have LEFT $<=$ RIGHT. We move LEFT as far to the right as possible without passing over any items larger than the pivot (where moving LEFT to the right involves adding 1 to LEFT). Then, by repeatedly subtracting 1 from RIGHT, we move it as far to the left as possible without passing over any values smaller than the pivot. If LEFT is strictly to the left of RIGHT, the items pointed to by LEFT and RIGHT are in the wrong order, so we switch them. After the switch, we move each index one position and resume the scanning until they cross, which has happened when LEFT $>=$ RIGHT. If we now swap the pivot (from position 1) with the item in RIGHT, we have the pivot item in its proper position, all data to the left of the pivot are smaller, and all data to the right are at least as large. Repeating this process on the segment to the right of the pivot, and then on the segment to the left of the pivot, we will eventually arrive at segments of length 1, which are in order and in the proper location. The specifics of the algorithm and a trace follow.

### *The Algorithm to Quicksort Array A (i) through A (j)*

```
pivot   <--   A (i)
LEFT    <--   i + 1
RIGHT   <--   j
repeat

  while (LEFT < RIGHT) and (pivot > A (LEFT))
       LEFT   <--   LEFT + 1

  while (LEFT <= RIGHT) and (pivot <= A (RIGHT))
       RIGHT   <--   RIGHT - 1

  if  LEFT < RIGHT
      then   temp   <--   A (LEFT)
             A (LEFT)   <--   A (RIGHT)
             A (RIGHT)   <--   temp
             LEFT   <--   LEFT + 1
             RIGHT   <--   RIGHT - 1

until LEFT >= RIGHT

temp   <--   A (RIGHT)
A (RIGHT)   <--   A (i)
A (i)   <--   temp

if  i < RIGHT - 1
    then quicksort (i, RIGHT - 1)

if  RIGHT + 1 < j
    then quicksort (RIGHT + 1, j)
```

### *A Trace of the Algorithm*

```
original data:        5  2  7  4  9  3  6  5  8
(pivot = 5)              L                    R
moving L and R:             L        R

1st swap:             5  2  3  4  9  7  6  5  8
(with move to L and R         L  R
moving L and R                R  L

pivot swap:           4  2  3  5  9  7  6  5  8
                               R

then:  quicksort (4  2  3), and
       quicksort (9  7  6  5  8)
```

When the two (shorter) quicksorts are done, the data will be sorted.

While this discussion certainly does not cover all of the algorithms for internal sorting or all of the variations on the algorithms outlined, it provides an adequate overview of internal sorting for the level of this course. In a later section we will come back to these algorithms and examine how efficiently they work. For now, however, let's look at the problem of sorting a data set that is too large to fit into an array structure contained in main memory.

## EXTERNAL SORTING

In external sorting, we are dealing with a large number of items, usually records in a data file. Because of the large number of records, and perhaps because of the length of each record, these records will not fit into a main-memory array. If the records need to be reordered into sequence on some field value, we can exploit the merging algorithm presented at the beginning of this chapter to perform our sort. If we do not need to physically arrange the records into the proper order but we do wish to access them in order, we might be better off using a pointer sort. These two approaches are presented here.

### Merge Sort

The merge sort is used to physically reorder the records in a data file, specifically, in situations where the file is too large to fit in main memory as an array structure (which is quite common for actual data files). The process involves taking our original file, which we can call file-1, and splitting it (as evenly as possible) into two temporary files (which we can call file-A and file-B). Taking blocks of length 1 from each file, we can "merge" these blocks into two more temporary files (say, file-X and file-Y). That is, we merge the first block (containing one record) of file-A with the first block of file-B into file-X, merge the second block of files -A and -B into file-Y, merge the third blocks and append the result to file-X, and then merge the fourth blocks and append to file-Y. We continue merging a block from file-A with a block from file-B, alternately appending the merged result to either file-X or file-Y, until all records from file-A and file-B have been processed. We now set the block size to 2, "clear out" the data in file-A and file-B, and merge each block from file-X with the corresponding block of file-Y, alternately appending the merged blocks (which have four records each) to file-A and file-B. This process continues, doubling the block size at each step, merging larger and larger blocks from one pair of temporary files into the other pair of temporary files, until we reach the point where we have only one block per file. The merge at this point will put all of the records into one file of the other pair and the second file of that pair will be empty. At this point, the records are in the proper order, so the temporary file can be renamed as file-O and the task is finished.

It should be noted that this is not a trivial operation in terms of either run time (because of the repeated file accesses and the file openings and closings) or storage space (because of the need for four temporary files), and therefore should not be done at the drop of a hat. However, if we in fact need to have a file physically sorted, the merge sort seems to be the best approach.

## Pointer Sort

Pointer sorting has a couple of advantages over merge sorting, but it has some disadvantages as well. The gist of this approach is to set up an array of pointers, one per data record in the file. Initially, the pointers each point to the corresponding record in physical order. That is, the pointer in position number 1 points to the location of the first record in the file, pointer number 2 points to record number 2, and so on. By means of a sorting algorithm, we will rearrange the pointers in the array so that they now follow the logical ordering of the records rather than their physical ordering. Thus our goal in the sorting process is to have the first position in the array point to the "smallest" record, the second position point to the second-smallest record, and so on. The actual sorting can be done with any of the sorting algorithms discussed previously, so long as the comparison tests of the algorithm are performed on the sort-field of the file and the data swapping operations of the algorithm are performed on the corresponding pointer-array elements.

The first advantage to pointer sorting is that pointers rather than data records are swapped. Particularly in cases where the records are fairly lengthy, this can provide a significant savings in run time. The second advantage is that we can sort the same data file on several different fields. By defining a pointer array for each desired sorting, we can access the data records in order by any of these attributes. For example, one array of pointers could give us employee records in alphabetical order, while another array of pointers could provide access based on length of employment (or salary, or whatever we wish). This could be accomplished at the same time that the records are physically stored in order by, say, Social Security number.

One disadvantage of pointer sorting is that the data file must be able to be accessed randomly by the location values stored in the pointer array. This means that the data file will probably need to have direct organization with relative addressing. Sequential or index-sequential organizations do not lend themselves to pointer access. The other main disadvantage, of course, is the extra storage space needed for the pointers. Whether the advantages outweigh the disadvantages depends on the circumstances.

## EFFICIENCY EVALUATIONS

We have raised the issue of run-time efficiency in several places during the course of this textbook, so perhaps we should conclude with a brief overview of how run-time efficiency is measured. This is of particular concern when the algorithm will have to deal with data sets of variable size, such as the sorting and merging algorithms that we have discussed here. Our concern is to see how the run time will be affected by increases in the number of data items to be handled. Generally speaking, we select one or more operations that have to be performed in our algorithm, and then get a rough count of how many times these operations can be expected to be done. Because of selection and iteration structures in the algorithm, the exact count will depend on the specific data values as well as on the number of items involved. We usually analyze the "average" case, where we consider reasonable probabilities that the selection and iteration control structures will choose one path over the other, although sometimes we also want to know about a worst-case scenario or perhaps even a best-case scenario. Also, since our main objective is usually to compare the rate of growth as the data set increases, we tend to simplify the formula for the count and focus on the dominant term of the expression. This will be illustrated shortly by considering the linear insertion sort algorithm. We will also present the efficiency results for the other sorting algorithms considered in this chapter.

In sorting, the two main operations to be considered are the comparisons and the data swaps. We will consider each of these independently of the other in our analysis. Looking back at the algorithm for linear insertion sorting, we see three iteration structures, two non-overlapping loops nested inside a third. The first inner structure contains one comparison test and the other contains one data move that represents a swap. The outer loop will execute $(n - 1)$ times, regardless of the data in the array. The first inner loop will execute anywhere from 1 to $k$ times, where $k$ is counting the executions of the outer loop. That is, on the fifth pass through the outer loop, the inner loop will execute from 1 to 5 times, depending on where the new item belongs in the sorted part of the list. We can safely assume that, on the average, the inner loop will execute $((k + 1)/2)$ times. Thus the total number of comparisons needed is expected to be the sum of $((k + 1)/2)$, where $k$ ranges from 1 to $(n - 1)$. Using calculations developed in either a discrete mathematics course or an algebra/calculus course, we can see that the average number of comparisons is $(n^2 + n - 2)/4$. Since in this analysis we are only concerned with the rate of growth, not the exact count, we can ignore the one-fourth. Also, since we are concerned with large values of $n$, we can ignore the terms of $n - 2$. Thus, the essence of the growth-rate estimate is $n^2$. The notation for this is $O(n^2)$, which is read as "big-oh of $n^2$." A more precise definition of the big-O notation can be found in the text by Aho, Hopcroft, and Ullman referenced at the end of this chapter.

A similar study of the data swapping in the linear insertion algorithm shows that the inner loop for the swaps will execute, on the average, $(k/2)$ times, with $k$ ranging from 1 to $(n - 1)$. The formula for the average number of swaps is then $(n^2 - n)/4$, which is again $O(n^2)$. Thus the linear insertion sort is an $O(n^2)$ algorithm. In particular, if we double the number of elements in the array to be sorted we can expect the algorithm to take approximately four times as long to execute, because $(2n)^2 = 4(n^2)$.

The ability to compute these run-time estimates is not one of the main objectives of a course in file processing at this level, so rather than develop run-time estimates for the other sorting algorithms, we will merely present the results here. Keep in mind that the larger the estimate, the more inefficient we can expect the algorithm to be on reasonably large data sets. Thus, in order of desirability, we have $O(1)$, $O(\log_2(n))$, $O(n)$, $O(n * \log_2(n))$, $O(n^2)$, and so on.

The binary insertion sort has $O(n * \log_2(n))$ comparisons because of the binary search for the proper location instead of the linear probing analyzed above. However, the number of data swaps will be exactly the same as for linear insertion, and hence will have $O(n^2)$. Thus, binary insertion is somewhat better than linear insertion, but not as good as some of the other sorts.

The Shell sort, as claimed above, does come out to be more efficient than linear or binary insertions. Depending on the spacing (denoted by $k$ in the discussion above), the average number of comparisons and the average number of swaps are between $O(n * (\log_2(n))^2)$ and $O(n^{1.5})$. (In order to see that $\log_2(n)$ grows more slowly than $n^5$, we would need to make use of L'Hospital's rule form calculus.)

The straight selection sort has $O(n^2)$ comparisons but only $O(n)$ moves (basically because each item in the array can move twice at most, once if it is bumped out of its original spot and once when it is put into its final spot). The bubble sort has $O(n^2)$ for both comparisons and swaps.

Quicksort is even more difficult to analyze because of the recursion involved. However, it has been shown that for randomly mixed data, quicksort is $O(n * \log_2(n))$ for both comparisons and swapping. Despite this, a worst-case analysis for quicksort, which occurs if the data are almost in correct order when starting, is $O(n_2)$ for comparisons and swaps. The heapsort, which was not presented here, overcomes this problem, and is an $O(n * \log_2(n))$ sort. Heapsort is also a recursive sorting algorithm.

## CONCLUDING REMARKS

In this chapter we have reviewed and extended some of the ideas of sorting normally covered in a freshman-level course in programming and data structures. We need to realize, however, that these issues of sorting and merging are typically no longer the domain of application programmers. Virtually all computer systems provide software to handle file merging and sorting for us. However, the principles and algorithms in this software are basically the same as what has been presented here.

## EXERCISES

1. Define *in situ* sorting.
2. Explain the difference between linear probing and binary searching.
3. Explain the difference between insertion sorts and selection sorts.
4. Explain why the bubble sort is a cross between an insertion technique and a selection technique.

5.  Explain in general terms how quicksort operates.

6.  Take the two lists of names given below and use them as the two input files to trace the merge algorithm.

    list A: Bob, Fred, John, Mark, Sam, Tom

    list B: Anne, Barb, Carrie, Julie, Sue, Tracy, Wendy, Zelda

7.  Use the list 5 2 9 1 7 6 4 3 8 to trace the execution of:

    a.  linear insertion

    b.  binary insertion

    c.  Shell sort

    d.  straight selection

    e.  bubble sort

    f.  quicksort

8.  Use the list 5 2 3 5 4 2 6 3 to trace each of the sorting algorithms listed in Exercise 7. When (if ever) do these algorithms encounter problems with duplicate data? What should be done to correct these problems?

9.  Use the list of values in Exercise 7 as record keys to trace the execution of the merge-sort for external sorting.

10. Using the list from Exercise 7 as record keys, set up the pointer array that would allow in-order access of these records without rearranging the relative positions of the records.

11. Verify the run-time estimates given for the bubble sort.

12. If our operation count turned out to be $5n^3 - 12n^2 + 17$, what would we take as our big-oh run-time estimate? What should we expect to happen to the run time if we double the value of $n$? What if we triple the value of $n$?

## PROGRAMMING PROJECTS

1.  Write a program that will take two files, each in proper order by primary key, and merge them into a single, properly ordered file. Your instructor will specify the type and size of the key, the size of the rest of the records, and the file naming conventions to be used.

2.  Write a program for each of the *in situ* sorts presented in this chapter. Your instructor will specify the protocol for supplying the

data to be sorted. If a large enough data set can be created and processed, you can time these programs to get a feeling for their relative efficiency. You can also see their relative efficiency on small data sets.

## OTHER READINGS

**1.**   Aho, A., Hopcroft, J., and Ullman, J. *Data Structures and Algorithms* (Reading, MA: Addison-Wesley Publishing Co., 1983).

**2.**   Aho, Hopcroft, and Ullman. *The Design and Analysis of Computer Algorithms* (Reading, MA: Addison-Wesley Publishing Co., 1974).

**3.**   Knuth, Donald. *The Art of Computer Programming,* vol. 3, *Sorting and Searching* (Reading, MA: Addison-Wesley Publishing Co., 1973).

**4.**   The Media Centre, University of Toronto. "Sorting Out Sorting" (thirty-minute video tape, 1981).

**5.**   Singh, B., and Naps, T. *Introduction to Data Structures* (St. Paul, MN: West Publishing Co., 1985).

# INDEX

## A

Access mode, 4
  direct, 5
  dynamic, 5, 10
  random, 5
  relative, 5
  sequential, 4
Actual addressing, 7, 51
Add transaction, 39
Addressing, actual, 7, 51
Addressing, direct, 7, 52
Addressing, indirect, 7, 52
Addressing, relative, 7, 52
Air cushion, disk drive, 115
Archive file, 3, 41
ASCII code, 8, 111
Audit, 4
Average search length, 70
AVL tree, 89

## B

B*-tree, 97
B$^+$-tree, 97
B$^+$-tree variations, 98
B-tree, 89
BACK external link, 60
Backup file, 2
  direct files, 68
  index-sequential files, 82
  sequential file, 47
Balanced tree, AVL, 89
Balanced tree, perfect, 89
Base conversion, 8
Batch processing, 3, 11

Batch updating, 39
Big-O notation, 159
Binary insertion sort, 148
Binary search tree, 84
  AVL, 89
  in-order traversal, 87
  perfectly balanced, 89
Block, disk, 114
Block, tape, 112
Blocking factor, 112
Bohm and Jacopini, 17
Bottom-up coding, 25
Bpi, 112
Branching control structure, 17
Bubble sort, 152

## C

Cache memory, 118
Case statements, 19
Catalog, database, 131, 138
Chained overflow, 10, 53
  implementation, 61
Chained progressive overflow, 73
Change format, coded, 40
Change format, positional, 40
Change transaction, 39
Changing primary key, 46
Channel, 119
Characteristics of a good program, 13
Child node, 84
Circular linked list, 57
CODASYL, 137
Coded change format, 40
Coding, bottom-up, 25
Coding, top-down, 25

**163**